Contents

Events in the Life of Alexander Graham Bell

1847

March 3, 1847
Alexander Bell is born to Alexander Melville Bell and Eliza Symonds Bell in Edinburgh, Scotland. He is the second of three sons. (He will adopt the name Graham at age eleven and become known as Alexander Graham Bell.)

April 1864
Alexander Melville Bell develops Visible Speech, a kind of universal alphabet of human voice sounds.

July 1870
Alexander Graham Bell emigrates with his parents to Canada after both his brothers die of tuberculosis.

Winter 1874–1875
Bell works on the harmonic telegraph in Boston with Thomas Watson while also teaching.

March 7, 1876
U.S. Patent No. 174,465 for "Improvements in Telegraphy" is issued to Bell.

Summer 1875
Bell and Watson construct the world's first telephone.

March 10, 1876
Bell hears Watson's voice over a liquid transmitter.

July 9, 1877
Bell, Watson, Thomas Sanders, and Gardiner Greene Hubbard form the Bell Telephone Company.

July 11, 1877
Bell marries Mabel Hubbard.

1879–1880
Bell works on the photophone with assistant Sumner Tainter after moving to Washington, D.C.

Summer 1881
Bell develops a telephone probe to assist mortally wounded President James Garfield.

1887
Helen Keller's father brings her to meet Bell, and the two become lifelong friends.

January 1888
Bell, Gardiner Hubbard, and others found the National Geographic Society.

August–September 1890
Bell and his supporters form the American Association to Promote the Teaching of Speech to the Deaf, which later changes to the Alexander Graham Bell Association for the Deaf and Hard of Hearing.

August 25, 1902
Bell discovers tetrahedral design, which leads to building a tetrahedral tower and experimental kites.

October 1, 1907
Glenn Curtiss, Thomas Selfridge, Casey Baldwin, Douglas McCurdy, and Bell form the Aerial Experiment Association (AEA) with funding from Mabel Bell.

March 12, 1908
Baldwin flies the *Red Wing*, the AEA's first powered aerodrome.

July 4, 1908
Curtiss flies the *June Bug* more than one kilometer.

February 23, 1909
McCurdy makes the first heavier-than-air flight in Canada in the *Silver Dart*.

January 25, 1915
Bell takes part in the formal opening of the transcontinental telephone line by talking on the telephone in New York to Watson in San Francisco.

August 2, 1922
Bell dies at his estate, Beinn Bhreagh, on Cape Breton Island, Nova Scotia, and is buried there. Mabel Bell dies five months later.

September 9, 1919
Bell and Baldwin's *HD-4* hydrofoil sets a world speed record of 70.86 mph.

1922

A Teacher and Inventor

*[I] was thus introduced to what proved to be my
life-work—the teaching of speech to the deaf.*

A tall, thin, serious-looking twenty-one-year-old man
with black whiskers stood at the classroom blackboard.
He wore a dark suit with a stiff collar and short necktie—
the standard outfit of a London professional in 1868. Four
young students sat in absolute silence, intently watching
their new teacher. But when Alexander Graham Bell
walked over to the children, they smiled and immediately
stretched out their open palms toward him. One by one,
instructor Bell took a small hand in his and began spelling
words into it. None of the four deaf students could hear a
sound. But Bell would teach them to speak.

As an old man, Bell would write about these early
lessons, saying he "was thus introduced to what proved to
be my life-work—the teaching of speech to the deaf." But
this young teacher became famous for a very different
kind of communication. In his late twenties, he invented a
device that instantly sent voices across thousands of
miles—the telephone. As fate would have it, Alexander
Graham Bell spent the better part of his life improving the
ways people communicated with one another. And in the
process, he became one of the most famous inventors of
all time.

CHAPTER 1

A Curious Kid

[M]y early passion for music had a good deal to do in preparing me for the scientific study of sound.

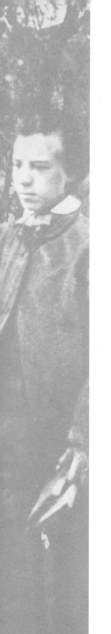

Warm, sunny days are not something to waste in rainy Scotland. One late-summer day in the early 1850s, a young family took advantage of the fine weather by spending time outdoors in the countryside. After they ate their picnic lunch, the boys ran off to play. The middle boy was named Alexander, and called Aleck. He was very young—only three or four years old. But Aleck was already fiercely independent.

A nearby wheat field swayed and shimmered. It caught Alexander's attention, and he set off to explore it. After entering the forest of tall wheat stalks, Aleck wondered: *Can you hear the wheat growing?* He sat for a long time and listened hard for sounds of growing wheat—without any

This photograph of eleven-year-old Alexander Graham Bell was taken by the boy's father in 1858 at the family's country home, Milton Cottage in Trinity.

luck. Then all of a sudden, the small boy realized he was lost. He had no idea how to get back to his family. The wheat was too tall to see over. Little Alexander panicked and began crying, finally sobbing himself to sleep in misery. "I was awakened by my father's voice," he later recalled. He sprinted in joy toward the sound of his father calling his name.

This was Alexander Graham Bell's earliest memory. But back then, he was simply Alexander Bell. He was born with no middle name on March 3, 1847, in Edinburgh, Scotland. He was named Alexander for his father and grandfather. But the three of them had more in common than just their names: Grandfather Alexander and father Alexander Melville were both expert communicators.

Alexander Graham Bell's paternal grandfather, Alexander Bell, sternly posed for this undated daguerreotype photograph.

Family Traditions

As a young man, Grandfather Alexander Bell was an actor; part of his training included elocution, the study of how to speak correctly. Being able to speak well is important for an actor, but Grandfather Bell discovered that it was actually his passion. He used what he learned in his voice training to teach students with speech problems such as stuttering.

In 1883, after Grandfather Bell and his wife divorced, his fourteen-year-old son Alexander Melville (called Melville) moved

Stuttering in the Nineteenth Century

Stuttering, also called stammering, is a speech disorder characterized by a broken flow of words or sounds. The interrupted flow can be involuntary sound repetitions, prolongations, hesitations, or complete stoppages. Sometimes the interrupted speech is accompanied by eyeblinks, head jerks, or other facial movements.

Stuttering usually shows up when a child first learns to speak and is more common in boys than girls. Scientists aren't sure what causes it, but genetics, developmental problems, and how a specific person's brain processes language can all influence stuttering. Stuttering can be treated by a speech therapist.

Grandfather Alexander Bell (1790–1865) lived during a time of much research into the causes and treatment of stuttering. In 1817, the French physician Jean Marie Itard claimed that a weakness of the tongue and larynx nerves caused stuttering and recommended exercises to cure it. Grandfather Bell himself weighed in with his book *Stammering and Other Impediments of Speech*, published in 1836. His treatment methods included training the stutterer in breath management and relaxation, as well as teaching the student how the vocal organs produced sounds so he or she could better control the process.

with him to London, England. There Melville went from assisting his father in his speech-tutoring business to being a talented speech teacher himself. But it was on a trip back to Edinburgh, Scotland, that twenty-four-year-old Melville Bell met the other love of his life. Her name was Eliza Symonds, an Englishwoman living in Scotland with her widowed mother. Eliza was thirty-four years old and nearly deaf. Melville Bell found her enchanting. He later wrote of their first meeting that Eliza had "the sweetest expression I think I ever saw. . . . She was so cheerful under her affliction that sympathy soon turned to admiration." Though nearly completely deaf since childhood, Eliza spoke and communicated well. She used an **ear tube** to help her hear, and she also read lips. She poured her energy into exploring the world through books, art, and music. She was also a talented portrait painter and pianist.

This photograph of the Alexander Melville Bell family was taken sometime between 1850 and 1860 at Milton Cottage. Pictured left to right are: Melville James (Melly), Alexander Melville, Edward Charles (Ted), Eliza, and Alexander Graham Bell.

Melville was in love, and he and Eliza were soon married. They settled in Edinburgh and had three sons—Melly, Aleck, and Ted. Melville Bell taught at the University of Edinburgh, published books on speech, and began working on something he called Visible Speech. It would become a universal alphabet of all the sounds a human voice can make.

Sound Beginnings

Eliza Bell was a talented woman in many fields, from painter to pianist, wife, and mother. And from the time her sons were old enough to read and write, she added another profession to her list: teacher. Eliza homeschooled her boys and also taught them the piano. Alexander took to the instrument with a passion. He quickly learned to read music and also to play piano by ear. Eliza Bell saw a special talent in him and hired a leading Edinburgh pianist to become his instructor. Auguste Benoit Bertini believed that Alexander was good enough to become a professional musician. Music filled young Aleck's head day and night.

When Alexander spelled out whole conversations to his mother, she didn't need to use her ear tube.

Melodies ringing in his mind kept him awake at night and left him with headaches in the morning. His mother called it "musical fever." But when his piano teacher died, the musical fever passed as well.

Aleck eventually lost interest in being a professional musician. But he enjoyed playing piano his whole life—often late into the night. Alexander Graham Bell later wrote that "my early passion for music had a good deal to do in preparing me for the scientific study of sound." It made him an expert listener with an ear that was sensitive to small differences in the tones and loudness of sounds. Studying, playing, and enjoying music also added to the special bond between Alexander and his pianist mother.

Eliza Bell listened to herself or others play the piano with her ear tube. She'd set its wide mouthpiece on the soundboard where the piano's strings were located. Then the narrow end of the ear tube went in her ear. This focused and carried the sound into her ear, like a funnel. When someone wanted to speak to Eliza, he or she would shout into the mouthpiece. But Alexander had his own, quieter way of communicating with his deaf mother. He learned that if he spoke to her in a low voice very close to her forehead, she could "hear" what he said. Young Alexander reasoned that she was actually feeling the vibrations of his speech, not hearing sounds. For Aleck, this was quite a breakthrough.

Eliza Bell also taught her middle son a finger-spelling alphabet made up of the speaker's hand positions placed on a listener's open palm. When Alexander spelled out whole conversations to his mother, she didn't need to use her ear tube. She could understand the words by feeling them spelled into her hand while also watching whomever was speaking.

An Inventive Youth

Edinburgh, Scotland, was a modern industrial city during

Alexander Graham Bell's father took this photograph of his second son c. 1861 when Aleck was fourteen or fifteen.

Finger-Spelling

Deaf people have been spelling out words manually for hundreds of years. Finger spelling uses hand positions to represent the letters of the alphabet. The voiceless speaker spells out words using the hand positions for a listener to see, or feel. There are many different finger-spelling, or manual, alphabets. Some are as simple as tracing out the shape of the letter in the air or on the palm. All the world's languages and scripts have their own distinct manual alphabets.

In the American finger-spelling alphabet system, letters of the English alphabet are formed by manipulating the fingers of one hand into specific positions and motions. The letters of the British finger-spelling alphabet are formed using two hands. The two-handed manual alphabet that Eliza Bell and her son used was similar to today's British finger-spelling alphabet, except that it was performed on the listener's palm. This freed the listener from having to watch the person finger spelling, and could also be used by deaf-blind people.

Alexander's youth. Steamships and trains sped passengers from place to place. Telegraph wires carried important messages, while factories and mills churned out goods. The city also brimmed with writers and scientists—many of whom frequented the Bell home. A number of inventions came out of Edinburgh, including the iron steamship and the pedal bicycle. It was an exciting time of new inventions that changed people's everyday lives—from photography to indoor toilets. The Bells were among those who believed that education and new technologies made life better for everyone.

Eliza Bell uses an ear tube to listen to her granddaughter while her husband, Melville Bell, eavesdrops in this 1884 photograph.

Life at the Bell home was fairly formal. The boys were expected to dress nicely and behave themselves indoors. But the Bells owned a country cottage in nearby Trinity where the boys could roam the hills in old clothes and even roll around in the dirt if they liked. Young Alexander spent his free time there collecting plants, studying animals, and riding an old-fashioned giant bicycle-like contraption called a velocipede. "Milton Cottage at Trinity was my real home in childhood," wrote Alexander Graham Bell looking back on those years.

Eliza Bell rides the family velocipede in this photograph taken c. 1859 at Milton Cottage. Aleck and his brothers, Melly and Ted, liked to pedal the vehicle around town.

Alexander liked his alone time. "In boyhood . . . I have spent many happy hours lying among the heather on the Scottish hills—breathing in the scenery around me with a quiet delight that is even now pleasant for me to remember," he later wrote. But Aleck spent time with friends, too. He'd met his friend Ben Herdman when Ben came to have his stutter corrected by Melville Bell. Ben's father owned an old mill nearby, and the two friends spent hours exploring and playing among the mill's stacked bags of flour and ancient grinding machinery.

One day, Alexander and Ben kept getting into mischief at the mill. Ben's father finally called them into his office and told them to find something useful to do. Alexander asked him what they might do that would be useful. After thinking a moment, the miller picked up a handful of harvested grain still covered in thick husks. "If only you could take the husks off this wheat, you would be doing something useful indeed," Mr. Herdman suggested.

The boys took up the challenge. First they tried scraping off the wheat husks with a stiff brush used to clean nails. It worked, but it took a long time by hand. They needed to make the work go faster.

Aleck remembered seeing a big vat, or tub, in the mill that had rotating paddles in it. He figured that if someone lined the wall of the vat

"Mr. Herdman's injunction to do something useful was my first incentive to invention, and the method of cleaning wheat the first fruit."

with stiff brushes, the paddles would push the grain against them and clean off their husks. "It was a proud day for us when we boys marched into Mr. Herdman's office, presented him with our sample of cleaned wheat, and suggested paddling wheat" in an old vat. The miller put the boys' idea into action—and it worked. Alexander's first invention was a success! Alexander Graham Bell wrote many years later, "Mr. Herdman's injunction to do something useful was my first incentive to invention, and the method of cleaning wheat the first fruit."

Careless Student

Like many middle children, young Alexander struggled to be noticed. He started with his name. To set himself apart from the other Alexanders in his family, he took the middle name Graham, after Alexander Graham, a family friend. He later explained that "Alexander Bell was not nearly substantial enough to suit me. So I chose the surname of one of my father's former pupils, who had come to board at our house, Alexander Graham. It had a fine strong sound to it." The family embraced his new middle name, toasting him with it on his eleventh birthday. But everyone continued to call him Aleck.

The family embraced his new middle name, toasting him with it on his eleventh birthday. But everyone continued to call him Aleck.

Alexander started Royal High School that year along with his younger brother Edward, called Ted. Their older brother Melville, known as Melly, already went there, and was the best student of the brothers. Alexander might have been a smart kid, but he wasn't a great student and didn't win any academic prizes. He was careless with math, hated learning Latin and Greek, and didn't even bother taking science classes. "I passed through . . . Royal High School . . . and graduated, but by no means with honors, when I was about fourteen years of age," Alexander Graham Bell would later write of his lackluster school days.

Melville Bell was not impressed with his middle son's poor efforts and lack of focus. Melville thought Alexander had to grow up and get serious about his future. And when Grandfather Bell wrote suggesting that Alexander come stay with him in London,

Aleck sits to the left of his younger brother, Ted, at Milton Cottage in this photograph taken between 1858 and 1862.

Melville decided that this was the push Alexander needed. So in the fall of 1862, fifteen-year-old Aleck left Edinburgh and got on a train bound for London, England. He would return a year later transformed into an ambitious young gentleman—Alexander Graham Bell.

CHAPTER 2

Becoming a Young Teacher

That year with my grandfather converted me from an ignorant and careless boy into a rather studious youth.

The first thing that Grandfather Bell did when his fifteen-year-old grandson arrived was call for a tailor. London, England, in 1862 was the bustling, sophisticated capital of the British Empire, after all. Grandfather Bell took it upon himself to transform his grandson into an educated upper-class Londoner—starting from the outside. One of London's best tailors soon had the teenager outfitted like a proper young gentleman. Whenever Alexander left his grandfather's Harrington Square home, he was dressed in a dark, tight fancy suit and tie, a top hat, gloves, and a cane!

Perhaps it was just as well that Alexander didn't have any young friends in London. He couldn't really hike and explore dressed up like a bridegroom. And there were no country hills in London anyway. Grandfather Bell kept Alexander too busy to miss his brothers and friends back in Scotland. Alexander was quickly put to work reading the plays of Shakespeare and other serious literature. He also studied speech with his grandfather, learning how to precisely pronounce each word he spoke. Alexander also sat in on many of his grandfather's sessions with his students, learning how to help those with speech problems.

Grandfather Bell was himself the son of a poor shoemaker. But his education helped him escape a dreary future and gave him the tools he needed to become a well-respected speech teacher. He firmly believed that education could help raise people out of a life of poverty and crime. This was a fairly radical idea in nineteenth-century England, where a person's social class

This photograph, taken between 1850 and 1860, shows a young Alexander Graham Bell seated between his father (right) and grandfather (left). The three shared the same first name.

was often set at birth. Alexander soaked up his grandfather's ideas along with his lessons during his year in London.

Grandfather Bell's impressive knowledge of all sorts of subjects made Aleck realize his own ignorance. Spending time with him gave the young man "the ambition to remedy my defects in education by personal study," as a grown-up Alexander later recalled. Grandfather Bell allowed Alexander free use of his library. Among the books the teenager found and read were some about sound. The once apathetic student now even began thinking about college.

> *Grandfather Bell's impressive knowledge of all sorts of subjects made Aleck realize his own ignorance.*

When his year was up and Melville came to take Alexander back to Edinburgh, he found that his son looked, spoke, and thought like an educated young gentleman. "That year with my grandfather converted me from an ignorant and careless boy into a rather studious youth," Alexander Graham Bell admitted. "From this time forth," he later wrote, "my intimates were men rather than boys, and I came to be looked upon as older than I really was."

A Speaking Machine

Before leaving for Scotland, Melville Bell went to visit a famous London scientist and took his son Alexander with him. Sir Charles Wheatstone was a physicist who had reconstructed and improved a speaking machine originally designed by Wolfgang von Kempelen. Melville Bell had heard about Wheatstone's speaking machine and wanted to see it for himself.

When the Bells arrived at the scientist's home, Wheatstone showed them a wooden box with an accordion-like bag on one

Sir Charles Wheatstone

Charles Wheatstone (1802–1875) was an English physicist and inventor known for his work on devices that measure electricity. Wheatstone also co-patented an early telegraph in England about the same time that Samuel Morse invented the telegraph in the United States.

Wheatstone invented the rheostat, a device that varies electrical resistance. It's what makes dimmer light switches work. The knighted scientist also invented the stereoscope, which is still used to view three-dimensional photographs today.

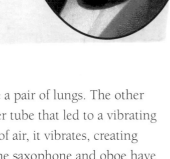

This undated image of Sir Charles Wheatstone shows the English physicist in later life. Teenage Alexander Graham Bell was impressed with Wheatstone's speaking machine.

side called a bellows, which acted like a pair of lungs. The other side of the box had levers and a leather tube that led to a vibrating reed. (When a reed is hit by a stream of air, it vibrates, creating sound. Musical instruments such as the saxophone and oboe have reeds, and are in fact known as instruments of the reed family.)

Wheatstone pushed on the bellows, sending air though the vibrating reed while squeezing the leather tube and working the levers. Out came words! The speaking machine's words sounded mechanical and crude, but Alexander was impressed by what he heard coming out of the box.

A year in London had matured Alexander into more than just a better student. The young man had tasted independence in his grandfather's home—and liked it. Melville Bell had sent his son an allowance every month, and Grandfather Bell had let Alexander spend it however he wanted. But back in Edinburgh, the allowance ended. Alexander felt "treated as a boy again, after I considered myself a man." Older brother Melly, too, grumbled about living under the rule of their father. Perhaps to distract his sons from revolt, Melville Bell challenged them to build a better, more human-like speaking machine.

After a lot of trial and error, Melly and Alexander put their halves together. Their speaking machine was ready to talk.

"My brother . . . and I attacked the problem together, and divided up the work," Alexander Graham Bell later recalled. "[Melly] undertook to make the lungs and throat of the **apparatus** while I made the tongue and mouth." Alexander used a real human skull as a model. He made the jaw and teeth out of hard rubber, cleverly creating a movable tongue and palate (roof of the mouth) out of small wooden slats covered in rubber that could be worked by levers. Alexander already knew that word pronunciation depended on how the tongue, lips, and mouth were shaped. Melly made the throat from a tin tube and the sound-producing voicebox, or larynx, out of two sheets of rubber that met at an angle. After a lot of trial and error, Melly and Alexander put their halves together. Their speaking machine was ready to talk.

The boys took their contraption out to the common

This photograph, taken sometime between 1850 and 1860, shows Alexander Graham Bell and his father at Milton Cottage. Melville Bell challenged Melly and Alexander to invent a speaking machine.

stairway in the house they shared with upstairs neighbors. Melly gave the machine lungs by blowing through the tin tube throat while Alexander maneuvered the lips, palate, and tongue. Out came a high whiny voice! After a little practice, they got it to say "mamma" like a baby. "'Mamma, Mamma' came forth with heart-rending effect," Bell remembered. "We heard someone above say, 'Good gracious, what can be the matter with that baby?,' and then footsteps were heard. This, of course, was just what we wanted. We quietly slipped into our house, and closed the door, leaving our neighbors to pursue their fruitless quest for the baby. Our triumph and happiness were complete."

Besides being a great practical joke, Alexander and Melly's speaking machine taught them a lot about how the human voice works. "The making of this talking-machine certainly marked an important point in my career," Alexander Graham Bell wrote in his sixties. "It made me familiar with the functions of the **vocal cords**, and started me along the path that led to the telephone."

Besides being a great practical joke, Alexander and Melly's speaking machine taught them a lot about how the human voice works.

Teacher and Student

Now that they'd conquered the speaking-machine challenge, Melly and Alexander went back to brooding about living at home. Edinburgh is a coastal city, and Alexander loved to visit its seaside docks and look out to the open ocean. A sailor's life seemed like a good idea—and a way to escape the rules and regulations of his parents' house. He packed up his clothes, intending to stow away on a ship. But at the last minute, Alexander had a change of heart. Perhaps a life at sea wasn't for him after all. He decided to look for a job on land instead.

A newspaper ad for pupil-teachers at a boys' boarding school soon caught Alexander's attention. In the 1800s, pupil-teachers often earned a higher education by teaching younger students while studying with the school's professors. Weston House Academy was one such school in Elgin, on the north coast of Scotland, 175 miles from Edinburgh. Alexander applied to teach music, and his brother Melly applied as a speech teacher. Eliza and Melville Bell didn't know their sons were even looking for jobs until the school's principal contacted Melville. The boys had listed him as a reference! A family meeting was called, and each boys' fate was decided. Melly would be sent to the University of Edinburgh for a year, while Alexander would go teach

This photographic portrait of Alexander Graham Bell was taken around 1865 while the eighteen-year-old was in Elgin, Scotland.

(and study) at Weston House Academy in Elgin.

So at sixteen Alexander Graham Bell left for Elgin and his first job, teaching music and speech. As payment, Alexander received a place to live, meals, Greek and Latin lessons, and ten pounds sterling per year (about 75 U.S. dollars). As it turned out, some of Alexander's students were older than he was! But they probably didn't realize it. Instructor Bell was a tall, serious, dark-haired young man clad in the finest London threads, including a top hat. No one mistook him for a boarding-school boy.

Seeing How to Speak

Alexander liked Weston and enjoyed exploring Elgin's caves and coast. In June 1864, at the end of his first teaching year, the young Bell's students impressed the Weston faculty during their final exams. The instructor who had been a mediocre student as a boy turned out to be an excellent teacher, and his students earned high grades.

Melville Bell had finished a universal alphabet of every sound of the human voice.

School was out until fall, so Alexander headed back to Edinburgh for the summer break. When he got home, he learned that he wasn't the only one having a big year. His father had finally solved a professional puzzle he'd been working on for fifteen years. Melville Bell had finished a universal alphabet of every sound of the human voice.

The first to learn the Visible Speech system were Melville Bell's three sons. Alexander alone mastered it in

Visible Speech

Visible Speech is a way to "read" sounds. It is a system of thirty-four symbols, called the Visible Speech alphabet. Each symbol represents a sound made by the human voice. It doesn't matter what language the sound comes from or even if it's part of a word. Sighs, sneezes, grunts, and coughs can also be written in the Visible Speech alphabet.

This page from Melville Bell's book *Class-Primer of English Visible Speech* shows words written in the Visible Speech alphabet.

Each symbol is like a code that informs a reader how to make the sound it represents. Different parts of each symbol tell how to shape the tongue, lips, throat, and mouth—the vocal organs—to produce a particular sound. For example, the horseshoe-like part of a symbol shows which part of the tongue to use. (Try to make the sounds *tee* and *guh* to see how differently your tongue is used.) A vertical line describes how open the throat is. (Try *eee* and *oh* as an example.) Once people learned the sounds of each symbol, they could pronounce any word or sound written in the Visible Speech alphabet. Even if a word was in a language they didn't know!

The Visible Speech system became an important tool in teaching the deaf to speak becuase it was not necessary to hear the sound to be able to speak it. Today language experts use a system of simpler symbols called the International Phonetic Alphabet. But Melville Bell's Visible Speech will always be the first. His historic book *Visible Speech: The Science of Universal Alphabetics* was published in 1867.

The Bells put on quite an impressive and entertaining show. But the most inspiring use of Visible Speech was yet to come.

five weeks. This helped when Melville set out on a lecture tour of Scotland with his boys. During demonstrations, one of his sons would first leave the auditorium. Then a volunteer from the audience would say something—often an unusual foreign word or phrase. Melville Bell wrote whatever the audience member said in Visible Speech symbols on the stage's blackboard. Next, the son returned and read the Visible Speech symbols aloud. He miraculously imitated whatever the audience member had said.

Alexander Graham Bell later wrote, "I remember upon one occasion the attempt to follow directions resulted in a curious rasping noise that was utterly unintelligible to me. The audience, however, at once responded with loud applause. They recognized it as an imitation of the noise of sawing wood, which had been given by an amateur ventriloquist as a test." The Bells put on quite an impressive and entertaining show. But the most inspiring use of Visible Speech was yet to come.

CHAPTER 3

Giving Voice to the Deaf

. . . I communicated to Mr. Ellis my discovery that in uttering the vowel elements of speech, faint musical tones could be heard accompanying the sound of the voice.

"What are you doing, Aleck?" asked Alexander's weary roommate. It was the middle of the night. But eighteen-year-old Alexander was across the room making faces in a mirror as he flicked a finger on his throat and cheek. Alexander's late-night activities had awakened his roommate at Weston House Academy.

While working on the Visible Speech system, Alexander and his father had debated why some vowel sounds were higher in pitch than others. Alexander wondered if there was a connection between pitch and the position of vocal organs. This was what Aleck told his roommate that night to explain his odd behavior. Alexander was listening to the changes in pitch, or musical tones, as he silently varied vocal positions and flicked a finger on his face. (Try it yourself. Silently shape your mouth as if you're saying *eee* and flick a finger against your cheek. Now try it with *oh*. Which sounds higher?) Alexander had discovered that it's the shape of the mouth and throat that create the different pitches of vowel sounds.

His next scientific step was to determine the precise pitch of each vowel sound. He used tuning forks of

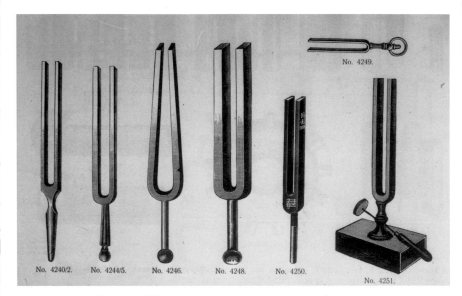

This woodcut illustrates different kinds of U-shaped tuning forks, all intended to tune instruments. Alexander Graham Bell used them to experiment with vowels and pitch.

different pitches to figure it out. Tuning forks are metal and shaped like a U with a handle on the bottom. They sing out particular pitches when struck, which is why they're used to tune instruments. Like anything that makes sound, a tuning fork sends sound waves into the air through vibrations. Alexander would strike a tuning fork, making it vibrate and sing out its particular pitch. While holding the singing tuning fork up to his mouth, he'd silently mouth the vowel sounds. If one of his mouth's vowel shapes made the tuning fork vibrate more—and therefore sound louder—Alexander knew that he'd found the vowel's pitch. This shared vibrating of sound is called resonance.

"Dear Papa," Alexander wrote his father from Elgin. "I have experimented again; and I find the general results of my former

The Bells' United Kingdom

Although Alexander Graham Bell was born in Edinburgh, Scotland, and spent his early childhood there, he traveled all over the United Kingdom as he matured into manhood. Young Alexander spent a year with his grandfather in London as a teenager, and his family moved to England's capital in 1865. Alexander Graham Bell was an instructor in Elgin, Scotland, and in Bath, England.

trial correct—and I now see the reason." Melville Bell encouraged his son to write up his findings and send them to the scientist Alexander John Ellis. "At the age of 18 years I communicated to Mr. Ellis my discovery that in uttering the vowel elements of speech, faint musical tones could be heard accompanying the sound of the voice," Alexander Graham Bell later wrote. Ellis was impressed and persuaded Alexander to join the London Philological Society, a group dedicated to

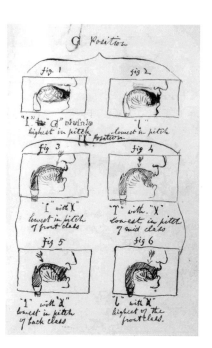

When Bell wrote to his father about his experiments in 1865, he included diagrams such as this one showing tongue positions within the mouth.

Hermann von Helmholtz

This engraving of Hermann von Helmholtz was made from a photograph taken in 1893, a year before the German physicist died.

Hermann Ludwig Ferdinand von Helmholtz (1821–1894) was a German physicist known for his discoveries and experiments with sound, including those that Alexander Graham Bell tried to repeat from Helmholtz's thesis *On the Sensations of Tone*. But Helmholtz is most famous for helping to establish the law of the conservation of energy. It states that energy can be neither created nor destroyed. Helmholtz also invented a number of medical instruments, including the ophthalmoscope, which doctors use to examine eyes.

the study of language and linguistics where he could pursue his love of language and speech. It was quite an honor for a teenager.

Tragedy and Change

By 1865, Grandfather Bell had passed away; his son, Melville, decided to move to London and continue his father's work. Meanwhile, Alexander took on a new teaching job at Somersetshire College in Bath, England, roughly one hundred miles from London. Besides teaching students and taking classes himself, Alexander kept experimenting. When the scientist Alexander John Ellis read Bell's report on vowel tones, he told the young experimenter that the famous scientist Hermann von Helmholtz had discovered the same thing. Bell already knew of

Helmholtz and was inspired that such a famous mind had pondered the same question. Ellis said that Helmholtz had gone further by causing tuning forks to continually vibrate and make vowel sounds by hooking them up to an electrical current.

Alexander Graham Bell wanted to try Helmholtz's experiments. But he needed to learn more about electricity. The electric lightbulb had not yet been invented, but there were electric motors and batteries. Best to learn by doing, Alexander decided. He filled his room in Bath with battery-making supplies—glass bottles, acid, zinc, and copper. Alexander and a friend in a nearby boardinghouse strung wires between their windows, hooked up telegraphs to each end, and started sending messages back and forth.

This photograph of Alexander Graham Bell's younger brother, Edward Charles (Ted), was taken in a photo studio sometime between 1860 and his death in 1867 from tuberculosis.

But things were changing in the Bell family. Back in London, Alexander's brother Ted was very sick. A bad cough turned out to be a disease that infects the lungs called tuberculosis. Ted was bedridden all winter, only able to sit up for an hour or so at time. "So long as Edward keeps still, he is not much troubled with his cough," Eliza wrote hopefully to Alexander around his twentieth birthday. But as everyone feared, Ted was just too sick. He died on May 17, 1867. "He was only eighteen years and eight months old," Alexander wrote in his diary that day.

Life in London

When the school year ended in 1867, Alexander moved home to London. He wouldn't be going back to Bath—even though he liked being independent. Ted was gone and Melly was now married, so Aleck was the only son at home. How could he abandon his parents?

It wasn't a terrible change. Alexander had plenty to do in London. He went to college at the University of London, and helped his father demonstrate his Visible Speech system. Audiences were amazed that Alexander could correctly pronounce a sound he'd never heard before by simply reading aloud the Visible Speech symbols. An old student of Melville's named Susanna Hull had a school for the deaf in London. When she learned about the Visible Speech system, she asked if it could be taught to her students. Twenty-one-year-old Alexander was sent by his father to try.

When Alexander Graham Bell arrived in the classroom, he picked up a piece of chalk and began sketching the outline of a face on the blackboard. He carefully drew a profile with a nose, lips, and jaw. Meanwhile, his students sat and watched in complete silence. There were only four children in the classroom, all girls under the age of ten. But they didn't blurt out questions or whisper to one another. The only sound in the classroom was chalk clicking and scraping across the blackboard.

Next, the young instructor filled in the profile with the insides of the mouth, such as the tongue and teeth. It was like looking at a cutaway view of the mouth's inside parts. Then Alexander walked over to the children. The girls immediately stretched their open palms out toward him. Finger spelling was how people talked to these children. Kate, Nelly, Lotty, and Minna couldn't hear voices or other sounds: All four girls were deaf. So Bell pointed to his blackboard drawing and finger-spelled *inside of mouth* into each petite palm.

The girls couldn't speak, either. It wasn't because there was something wrong with their voices. They could cry, scream,

He believed that if the deaf could learn how to make the sounds of the alphabet, they could string those sounds together and speak words.

and make noises. But forming actual words was different. Babies and toddlers learn to speak by listening and copying the words they hear. But babies and toddlers who are deaf can't copy sounds. In the mid–nineteenth century, many believed it was impossible to teach the deaf to speak. Alexander Graham Bell disagreed. He believed that if the deaf could learn how to make the sounds of the alphabet, they could string those sounds together and speak words.

So how do you teach a deaf person to speak? You show her how to shape her mouth and tongue so it makes the appropriate sound. This was why Bell was drawing the insides of a mouth on the blackboard. He was letting his students see how to position their mouths and tongues. He was letting them see sounds in the making.

Seeing Sounds and Speaking Success

In the little classroom, the girls learned fast. They each touched their tongues, lips, and throats as Bell pointed out those parts on the blackboard mouth. They learned that these were the parts involved in forming speech. Next, Bell drew a mouth making a particular sound, such as the *kuh* sound. The girls learned to say "kuh" by shaping their mouths like the picture. Bell helped them practice the sound until they could speak it correctly. Then they learned another. And another.

This early 20th-century lithograph depicts Alexander Graham Bell instructing a deaf student. Bell considered teaching the deaf to speak the most important work of his life.

By the end of their fifth lesson, the girls were beginning to master the alphabet. But individual letters sound differently depending on what words they're in. For example, the *c* in *cat* sounds very different from the *c* in *cent*. But that was no problem for an expert like Bell. He came to class armed with thirty-four symbols that represented very specific vocal sounds. He was using his father's Visible Speech alphabet, which translated each symbol into a particular sound. The students could learn how to pronounce a word like *cat* correctly without having to hear it.

Kate, Nelly, Lotty, and Minna worked hard with their dedicated teacher. They desperately wanted to learn to speak.

Soon eight-year-old Kate was able to say for the first time, "I love you, Mama." Teaching at the deaf school was the beginning of what Alexander Graham Bell would consider to be his lifework—teaching the deaf to speak. The young instructor quickly earned a reputation as a talented teacher of the deaf.

Death and New Beginnings

Alexander's young adult life was coming together nicely. Besides teaching and studying, he took care of his father's speech business while Melville Bell was away. Melville had traveled to North America to promote Visible Speech. While there, he visited old friends who'd moved to Canada from Scotland. Melville liked Canada and thought about moving there, too, but for now he felt he belonged in London.

Yet death always has a way of bringing change. The Bell family was no exception, and illness hung over brother Melly Bell's Edinburgh home. He and his wife, Carrie, sent a picture of their son, Edward, to London. It showed a "determined little fellow" with big eyes and clenched fists. But baby Edward wasn't well. And Melly was thin and pale, too. In early 1870, baby Edward died at just over a year old—of tuberculosis. The loss caused Melly to take up spiritualism, the belief that the living could communicate with the dead through meetings called séances. Melly made his brother Aleck promise that whoever died first would try to communicate with the other.

Yet death always has a way of bringing change. The Bell family was no exception . . .

Melly died of tuberculosis at age twenty-five on May 28, 1870. He was buried beside his brother Ted and Grandfather

Consumed by Tuberculosis

In this 1901 illustration, a woman with tuberculosis is being treated with electricity. The tuberculosis epidemic spawned all kinds of bizarre treatments for the disease, some helpful and others harmful.

Tuberculosis, or TB, is a disease caused by a type of bacteria that infects the lungs. Today people with TB are usually cured with antibiotics and other drugs that fight bacteria. But there were no such medicines during Alexander Graham Bell's time. Tuberculosis ravaged Europe and North America; it was the leading cause of death in the 1800s. People called it consumption, because TB slowly consumed and weakened the bodies of its victims over time. Someone with TB might spend months in bed wasting away before finally dying.

Tuberculosis spreads easily when someone coughs or sneezes. So those who lived close together in unhealthy cities were even more likely to catch the disease. Open sewers, contaminated water, and soot-belching factories polluted the air, and food spoiled without refrigeration. Recovery homes for TB patients called sanitariums opened in the late 1800s to help cure patients with fresh air, rest, and good nutrition. Sanitariums also kept infected people from passing on the disease to others.

He kept his promise of trying to communicate beyond the grave.

Bell in London. The death of his older brother devastated Alexander. "I well remember how often—in the stillness of the night—I've had little séances all by myself in the half-hope, half-fear of receiving some communication," he later wrote. He kept his promise of trying to communicate beyond the grave, though without success.

After burying two sons, Eliza and Melville Bell began to seriously worry about Alexander's health. He was awake half the night and asleep all morning. He often complained of bad headaches. Would the Bells' only remaining son succumb to tuberculosis, too? A trip to the doctor added to their fears. The doctor claimed that if Alexander didn't move someplace healthier to recuperate, he'd likely die in six months or so. Eliza and Melville felt that Canada was the cure Alexander needed. But could they convince him to go?

This photograph of Alexander Graham Bell's older brother, Melville James (Melly), was taken sometime in the decade before his 1870 death from tuberculosis.

Alexander felt his dream of an independent life falling apart around him. If he moved to Canada, he'd never finish his college degree, and he'd have to leave his students at the deaf school. But how could he say no to his parents? They'd already lost two sons. Alexander was their only living child. He felt it was his duty to fulfill his parents' wishes. In a letter to his father, Alexander wrote that his dream of independence "has perished with poor Melly. It is gone and for *ever* . . . [and] I have *now* no other wish than to be near you, Mama . . . and I put myself unreservedly into your hands to do with me whatever you think for the best." It was signed, "Your affectionate and *only* son, Aleck." A ship soon carried Alexander and his family away from the British Isles and across the Atlantic Ocean. It landed in Canada on August 1, 1870. Alexander Graham Bell had arrived in North America.

But how could he say no to his parents? They'd already lost two sons.

CHAPTER 4

The Bell Patent Association

At once the conception of a membrane speaking telephone became complete in my mind.

After moving to Canada from London, Alexander Graham Bell spent most of a year at the Bells' new family home in Brantford, Ontario. The house overlooked the Grand River, and Aleck soon found a restful spot where the river rolled by below. "It was my custom in the summer time to take a rug, a pillow, and an interesting book to this cozy little nook and dream away the afternoon," he later wrote. The Canadian country climate had delivered the cure Eliza and Melville Bell had hoped for. The health of their only living child was restored.

Once he recovered, Alexander moved to Boston, Massachusetts, in 1871 to instruct teachers of the deaf on how to use Visible Speech. This move proved to be a good decision for the ambitious young instructor. Within a couple of years, Alexander Graham Bell had advanced from a teacher of the deaf at a number of schools to a professor of **vocal physiology** at Boston University. Newspapers reported on the amazing progress young Professor Bell made in teaching deaf students to speak using Visible Speech. Like the Alexander Bells before him, Alexander Graham Bell also opened his own speech-tutoring business. He called it Bell's School of Vocal Physiology.

Early Bostonian Experiments

Bell continued to experiment with sound—with the help of an instrument called a phonautograph. Invented in 1857 by Léon Scott de Martinville, the phonautograph was the first instrument to record sound. But it didn't record the sounds themselves. Instead, it made "sound pictures" by tracing the patterns of sound waves on paper.

Bell thought a machine that drew sounds would be a great tool for deaf students. If they could see the correct pattern of a

The Phonautograph

This wood engraving, c. 1870, depicts a demonstration of an early phonautograph, the first device to record sound. It was invented by Léon Scott de Martinville in 1857.

The first phonautograph was made of a cone-shaped mouthpiece covered with a thin **membrane**. Someone would speak into the mouthpiece, and his or her voice would create sound waves. These sound waves caused the thin membrane to vibrate. A needle attached to the membrane moved up and down with the vibrations, scratching the vibrations' patterns—sounds—on coated glass plates. A visual picture of the sound was thus created.

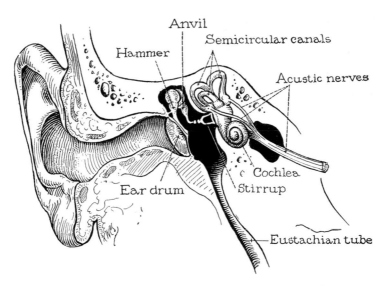

This diagram of the ear's anatomy shows how vibrations from the eardrum affect the ear bones—hammer, anvil, and stirrup—because of how close they are to each other. Bell built a phonautograph using a real human ear because of the sensitivity of the earbones.

word made by a phonautograph, they would know that their own pronunciation of the word was correct when they created a vocal pattern that matched it.

Unfortunately, phonautographs weren't sensitive enough to show small but important differences in pronunciation. Not ready to admit defeat, however, Bell built a phonautograph as sensitive as the human ear—using a real human ear from a corpse! He attached a thin straw to one of the tiny bones inside the ear. Then he mounted the ear over a piece of soot-coated glass. When someone spoke into the ear, the **eardrum** vibrated, set the ear bones in motion, and caused the straw to trace lines on the glass.

Alexander Graham Bell never made a workable teaching tool for deaf students out of his human ear phonautograph. But it "paved the way for the appearance of the first membrane telephone," the inventor later wrote. How? It showed that sound waves caused vibrations strong enough to power an instrument like the phonautograph. What else might spoken sound waves be strong enough to power? The answer was the other subject of Bell's early Boston experiments—electrical current.

Building a Better Telegraph

Boston in the late nineteenth century was a city full of scientists, universities, and wealthy investors willing to finance new instruments of technology. One such man was Gardiner Greene Hubbard, a successful lawyer.

Hubbard's daughter, Mabel, was deaf, and was a student of Alexander Graham Bell's. Hubbard liked the young professor, and Bell was often a guest in the Hubbard home. In the fall of 1874, during one such visit, Bell entertained the family with his fine piano playing. Suddenly he stopped playing and spun around on the piano stool toward his hosts. He asked if they knew that a piano could sing back at you. To show what he meant, he pressed down the foot pedal that gives the piano's strings slack, and loudly sang a note into the instrument. As promised, the

This photograph, c. 1895, of wealthy Boston lawyer and financier Gardiner Greene Hubbard was taken late in his life.

piano sang out the exact same note—as if someone had struck a piano key! The trick was caused by the same resonance that Bell had experimented with using tuning forks.

Gardiner Greene Hubbard asked young Bell if his trick had any practical use. Bell explained that the principle could be used to send several telegraph messages over a single wire at the same time. Hubbard excitedly realized that his guest was talking about a multiple telegraph—something inventors had been desperately trying to invent for many years. And Bell was one of them. A

Bell called his idea for a multiple telegraph a "harmonic telegraph."

newspaper article he'd once read mentioned the inventors' struggle, and it made Bell realize that the experiments he'd done with sound and electricity might be the key to this important invention.

Bell called his idea for a multiple telegraph a "harmonic telegraph." It could be done if each message had its own separate pitch, Bell reasoned. The differently pitched messages could all be sent together, much the way a musical chord on a piano plays multiple notes. Tuning forks of various pitches could send out the messages across a telegraph wire simultaneously. Different tuning forks on the receiving end of the wire would pick up the messages sent in their same pitch. This would then unjumble the messages into separate streams of Morse code.

Hubbard listened carefully while Bell explained his harmonic telegraph idea. Little did Bell know that Hubbard wanted nothing more than for someone to invent the next step in telegraph technology to loosen Western Union's **monopoly**. Then maybe telegraph prices would drop—to the benefit, Hubbard felt, of all American businesses. How amazing that the man to do it might be right here in his home!

The Telegraph

The telegraph was an instrument that sent messages using an electrical current over wires. A telegraph operator sent signals over a wire by interrupting the flow of electrical current. The message was made up of shorter and longer bursts of current, known as Morse code, which represented letters of the alphabet. A receiver then decoded the long and short clicking sounds into a written message.

Samuel Morse invented the first practical telegraph in 1837. By the 1850s, it had become an important way to communicate news, business information, and the movement of railroad trains. By the 1860s, most cities had telegraph offices, and telegraph wires strung across the world. Both the Union and Confederate armies communicated via telegraph during the American Civil War.

On May 24, 1844, Samuel Morse sent the first telegraph message—"What hath God wrought?"—from Washington, D.C., to Baltimore on the telegraph machine shown above.

This 1881 illustration shows the busy central operating room of the Western Union Telegraph Company. Rows of operators sit at telegraphs sending messages in code.

At first, there were many telegraph companies, each with its own lines and message offices. But many were unreliable and failed. By 1866, one company had gained control of most of the United States—the Western Union Telegraph Company. While Western Union's monopoly helped improve the chances that a message would actually get from one place to another, getting it out was still a long, dreary process. You had to go to an office, give an operator your message, and wait for it to be sent. And since only one telegraph message could travel along a wire at a time, you could be in for an awfully long wait. Needless to say, Western Union was desperate to find a way to send multiple messages at once. After all, the more messages sent, the more money made!

Gardiner Greene Hubbard quickly seized this rare opportunity. He offered to fund Bell's experiments in exchange for a share of any invention's profits. Bell had already had a similar offer from another parent of a student, Thomas Sanders. The result was a three-way partnership among Thomas Sanders, Gardiner Greene Hubbard, and Alexander Graham Bell. The two wealthy men would pay the inventor's expenses, and they'd divide the profits of any successes three ways. The group later earned the name the Bell Patent Association.

Daydreams of a Speaking Telegraph

Alexander Graham Bell thought his harmonic telegraph idea was good. But though its success promised fame and fortune, it wasn't what he really wanted to invent. Whether telegraph messages were sent one at a time or ten at a time, they were still just crude strings of signals that had to be translated into words by an operator. Wouldn't it be better to send the spoken words instead? What Alexander Graham Bell really wanted to invent was a speaking telegraph—the telephone. Just how a telegraph could be made to carry voice sounds came to Bell during summer break in 1874, at his parents' Brantford, Ontario, home. The vacationing professor soon found himself resting in a familiar spot, his "dreaming place" above the Grand River.

Bell watched the river roll by and daydreamed. His thoughts wandered from the piano parlor trick to experimenting with electricity. Then his mind bounced from his deaf students to the ear phonautograph he'd made. The sound wave tracings made by the phonautograph looked like smoothly snaking lines. The tracings had an unbroken, up-and-down pattern. This continual undulating line pattern created by speaking into a phonautograph proved to Bell that a regular telegraph could never carry the human voice. Why? The clicking sounds that make up telegraph code are created by stopping and starting electrical current. The telegraph's current

In this 1917 photograph, an elderly Alexander Graham Bell and his daughter stand in front of his parents' home in Brantford, Ontario, where the inventor made some important discoveries as a young man.

has to be interrupted, completely unlike the continual sound waves of the voice shown by the phonautograph. Bell also knew that as sound waves travel, the pockets of air they pass through compress and expand. But the ear phonautograph's ability to scratch ink on glass had proved to him that voice sounds were powerful— maybe even powerful enough to control an electrical current. And then he knew how a telephone could work.

Bell just had to find out if his idea worked—by building it.

Bell later wrote that he realized, "It would be possible to transmit sounds of any sort if we could only . . . [vary] . . . the current exactly like that occurring in the density of air while a given sound is made." And from his experiments with electricity, Bell reasoned that a vibrating magnet could create just the right kind of varying, undulating current. Electricity could carry tones—and the human voice! But how could he get a heavy magnet to vibrate with the small changes in air density caused by voice sounds? His ear phonautograph held the answer again. Its human eardrum moved the ear bones through vibration. A bigger, thicker membrane could be made to move a metal magnet the same way. "At once the conception of a membrane speaking telephone became complete in my mind." Alexander Graham Bell just had to find out if his idea worked—by building it.

CHAPTER 5

Love and Work

*I have discovered that my interest in my dear pupil
. . . has ripened into a far deeper feeling.*

Thomas Watson liked his job at the electrical shop where
he worked making telegraph and fire alarm equipment.
As one of the shop's best machinists, twenty-year-old
Watson did custom work for inventors. The grimy
workbenches covered in bits of metal, wire, wood, and
every tool imaginable were like paint and canvas
to him. He could create any kind of
electrical device a customer asked
for. "I made stubborn metal do my
will and take the shape necessary
to enable it to do its allotted
work," Watson recalled.

One day in 1874, Watson
looked up from his workbench to
see a gentleman customer rushing
through the office and into the
shop. *That's odd*, thought Watson.
Customers were supposed to first

Thomas Watson first met Alexander Graham Bell in
1874, the same year this photograph of the
machinist, then twenty years old, was taken.
The partnership would make Watson
both wealthy and famous.

talk to someone in the office, not just walk into the shop. Watson remembered the visitor as "a tall, slender, quick-motioned young man with a pale face, black side-whiskers and drooping mustache, big nose and high, sloping forehead crowned with bushy jet-black hair."

The impatient customer was twenty-seven-year-old Alexander Graham Bell. The Boston University professor walked right up to young Watson and began quizzing him about different devices. Bell knew that he needed the help of a skilled craftsman if he was ever going to build a working invention. "I . . . was always clumsy in the use of my hands and inefficient where tools were concerned," Bell wrote. Thomas Watson was just the help Alexander Graham Bell needed. Watson soon started working with Bell on his inventions, and their work relationship grew into a deep friendship, too. "No finer influence than Graham Bell ever came into my life," Watson wrote. Little did Alexander Graham Bell and Thomas Watson know that their partnership would go down as one of the most important in the history of inventions!

Pressure and Advice

Alexander Graham Bell now had mechanical help from Thomas Watson and financial help from the Bell Patent Association. A patent is an official government document that allows only the inventor to make, use, or sell that particular invention. A patent protects an inventor's idea from being stolen. The pressure was turned up on Bell to quickly invent and patent his multiple harmonic telegraph idea. Time was running out. Other inventors were working on their own multiple telegraph designs. If they got their inventions working and patented first, the Bell Patent Association would lose all of its investment money, instead of gaining a fortune.

Thomas A. Watson

Machine shops like the one Thomas Watson worked in were essential to inventors, because in the nineteenth century metal parts had to made individually by hand. This photograph, c. 1900, shows two men working at a lathe.

Thomas Augustus Watson (1854–1934) was born in Salem, Massachusetts. His father ran a livery stable, a place that rented out horses and carriages. Watson left school at age fourteen, restless and bored with classwork. He drifted from job to job, trying to find something he liked. At eighteen, Watson started working at a machine shop in Boston. Not only did he enjoy the work, but he proved to be very good at making electrical machines and devices for the shop's customers—some of whom were inventors like Alexander Graham Bell.

After helping Bell invent the telephone, Watson became a wealthy man. He went on to start a successful shipbuilding business that grew into the largest in America. Never one to stop learning, Watson also studied geology and paleontology and had a group of fossil snails named for him! Later in life, Thomas Watson turned to acting and playwriting. He also lectured about the telephone and wrote his autobiography, titled *Exploring Life*, which was published in 1926.

Alexander Graham Bell and Thomas Watson toiled at the harmonic telegraph in an attic workshop all that winter. Despite the pressure, Bell never stopped thinking about his idea for a speaking telegraph, the telephone. It was still the invention that haunted him. No one would want a crude dot-and-dash code telegraph once voices could travel along wires, he reasoned. But Bell's harmonic telegraph was what the Bell Patent Association was backing him to invent. The multiple telegraph was the first race to win.

By late winter of 1875, Watson and Bell had made some progress. Hubbard and Sanders sent their inventor off to file patents on the harmonic telegraph technologies developed so far. Alexander Graham Bell boarded a train for Washington, D.C., and the U.S. Patent Office. While in the nation's capital that March, Bell paid a visit to the famous scientist Joseph Henry at the Smithsonian Institution. Henry had made many discoveries about electricity and **electromagnetism**. He'd also worked on telegraph technology, and his ideas had helped Samuel Morse invent the telegraph. Perhaps Henry would be interested in his inventions, Bell thought.

The Smithsonian Institution sits halfway between the Washington Monument and the Capitol building in Washington, D.C. Alexander Graham Bell was no doubt intimidated meeting the famed scientist in such a

Joseph Henry was a physicist who made many discoveries about electricity and electromagnetism. He posed for this photograph between 1860 and 1875 when he was director of the Smithsonian.

prestigious setting. The elderly physicist seemed uninterested in Bell's description of the harmonic telegraph. But Henry's interest perked up when Bell demonstrated some of the electrical equipment that he and Watson had built. Feeling a bit more relaxed and respected, Bell risked telling the esteemed scientist his other idea for an invention—the telephone.

After explaining to Henry how a device might be able to carry voices with electricity, Bell asked the physicist for advice:

The Smithsonian Institution

In 1829, British scientist James Smithson left his fortune to the U.S. government to found an establishment for the "increase and diffusion of knowledge among men." Congress chartered the Smithsonian Institution in 1846 in Washington, D.C. The most revered American scientist of the time, Joseph Henry (1797–1878), was appointed its first director. Today the Smithsonian Institution is a nonprofit organization of scientific, educational, and cultural interests and includes more than a dozen museums, the National Zoo, and *Smithsonian* magazine.

This photograph of the Smithsonian Institution when Joseph Henry was its director was taken between 1861 and 1864. A fire destroyed parts of the original building in 1865.

Should he publish his idea now and leave the inventing to others? Joseph Henry had himself missed out on a number of inventions by not patenting his own ideas early enough. Perhaps he hoped this young inventor wouldn't repeat his own mistake. "[Henry] said he thought it was 'the germ of a great invention' and advised me to work at it myself," Bell wrote in a letter to his parents. When Bell complained to Henry that he didn't really have the electrical expertise, the seventy-seven-year-old physicist scolded, "Get it!" "I cannot tell you how much these two words have encouraged me," the young man wrote his parents. Bell would later admit, "But for Joseph Henry, I would never have gone ahead with the telephone."

Bell would later admit, "But for Joseph Henry, I would never have gone ahead with the telephone."

Love and Threats

"Every moment of my time is devoted to study of electricity and to experiments," Bell wrote his parents that spring of 1875. "I think the transmission of the human voice is much more nearly at hand than I supposed."

Back at work in Massachusetts on the harmonic telegraph with Watson, Bell shared his "other idea" with his friend and partner. "Watson, if I can get a mechanism which makes a current of electricity vary in its intensity, as the air varies in density when a sound is passing through it, I can telegraph any sound, even the sound of speech," Bell explained. He was now convinced that the telephone would be a much more important invention than any kind of dot-and-dash-sending telegraph!

Gardiner Greene Hubbard disagreed with Alexander Graham Bell about the telephone. To the wealthy lawyer, the telephone was too futuristic, an impossible dream. Even if it was invented, Hubbard had no proof that anyone would want one. But he knew without a doubt that Bell's invention of a multiple telegraph would earn them all a lot of money. The choice was obvious. Hubbard demanded that Bell not work on a "talking by wire" invention. Bell was therefore forced to delay his dream.

The conflict between Bell and Hubbard was about to get a lot more complicated. After years spent as Mabel Hubbard's teacher and dinner guest—and even an employee of her father's—Bell had fallen in love with her. Their tutoring sessions had turned into long discussions of politics and culture. Alexander found Mabel warm, caring, and intelligent. As was proper for the time, he wrote seventeen-year-old Mabel's parents a letter that told them of his feelings for their daughter and asked permission to "court" or date her. "I have discovered that my interest in my dear pupil . . . has ripened into a far deeper feeling," twenty-eight-

After years spent as Mabel Hubbard's teacher and dinner guest—and even an employee of her father's—Bell had fallen in love with her.

Mabel Hubbard could not hear, but she could speak and read lips in multiple languages. This photograph of her was taken in July 1877.

This photographic portrait of Mabel Hubbard as a toddler was taken c. 1860, before scarlet fever took away her hearing at age five.

Mabel Hubbard could hear normally for the first five years of her life. But then a bad case of **scarlet fever** took away her hearing. High fevers in children can damage the nerves crucial for hearing. Mabel already talked at five and continued to speak even after losing her hearing. But over the years of silence, her speech muddied and grew harder for people to understand—especially strangers.

And for Mabel, meeting strangers could be very difficult. They often ignored her after they found out she was deaf. But Mabel could read lips—in several languages! She painfully understood every rude comment made about her. The dark-eyed teenager with long hair didn't want their pity; she wanted to be treated as an equal.

When Mabel met Alexander, her new tutor, she was doubtful that he could help her speak. Her wealthy parents had already hired tutors for her in America and Europe, but none had really helped her speak more clearly. When they met in 1873, Mabel Hubbard wasn't very impressed with Professor Alexander Graham Bell. The wealthy, European-educated teenager complained in her diary that "he dressed badly and carelessly in an old-fashioned suit." But Professor Bell's teaching soon won Mabel's respect. A few months later, just after Mabel turned sixteen, she wrote her mother that her speech was already greatly improved. Alexander Graham Bell, on the other hand, was immediately impressed with Mabel Hubbard. She was intelligent, interested in the world around her, and a hardworking student. He also thought Mabel poised and strikingly beautiful.

year-old Bell wrote. The Hubbards did not approve. They asked Alexander to keep his feelings from Mabel secret for a year. Then she'd be older and able to decide for herself about a suitor.

Alexander suffered in silence that summer until his secret escaped to Mabel through a gossiping cousin. In a volley of letters, Alexander opened his heart to Mabel, writing of "my wish to make you my wife—if you would let me try to win your love." Mabel answered honestly, telling Alexander that she respected him greatly as her tutor. But she did not love him—nor was she even sure what love was yet. Bell was actually encouraged by her answer! *At least she didn't reject me completely*, he thought. He kept writing her, and Mabel Hubbard finally agreed to be courted by Alexander Graham Bell.

Bell needed to make a living—especially now that he had marriage on his mind. With all the time he'd spent on the harmonic telegraph, he'd neglected his tutoring business. But when he started spending more time teaching Visible Speech and less working on the harmonic telegraph, Gardiner Greene Hubbard hit the roof. Hubbard told Bell that the competition was going to beat them to the invention because of the young man's lack of focus. The financial backer of his inventions and the father of the young woman he loved gave Alexander Graham Bell an astonishing **ultimatum**: Either give up his career teaching the deaf, or give up Mabel and inventing. The choice was Bell's.

CHAPTER 6

Mr. Watson—Come Here

The speaking telephone was born at that moment.
　　—Thomas Watson

High temperatures didn't agree with wool-suited Scotsmen such as Alexander Graham Bell. The heat gave him headaches and made him irritable. June 2, 1875, was one such hot, frustrating day. The attic workshop where Bell and Thomas Watson had worked all day was sweltering. The men were testing the harmonic telegraph invention—and it wasn't going well. "In spite of Bell's hard study on his telegraph invention . . . we couldn't make it work rightly," wrote Watson.

Bell and Watson were trying to get their harmonic telegraph to simultaneously send three telegraph messages by making all three electrical signals a different pitch. Bell had abandoned the idea of using tuning forks to shuttle the precise pitches. Now thin strips of steel called reeds vibrated and sang out the harmonic telegraph's tones. Bell and Watson were painstakingly adjusting the screws that held the reeds down that steamy June evening when something strange happened.

As they'd done time and again, Watson stationed himself in the room with the **transmitters** and tried to send multiple messages to Bell, who was in another room with the **receivers**. When one of Watson's transmitter reeds got stuck and quit vibrating, he tried freeing the strip of metal. "I began to readjust the screw while continuing to pluck the reed, when I was startled by a loud shout from Bell," wrote Watson. Bell came running in, asking Watson what he had done!

The reed on Bell's receiver end had vibrated with Watson's plucking, singing out twangs of sound. Bell recognized the faint sound as more than a simple telegraph signal. He realized that the plucked reed's vibrations had varied the electrical current, and that the receiver's reed had reproduced the same sound-shaped electrical current. It was just as Bell had dreamed up the summer before. If electricity could transmit this complex sound, Bell knew it could transmit the human voice.

If electricity could transmit this complex sound, Bell knew it could transmit the human voice.

Alexander Graham Bell's famous workshop at 5 Exeter Place in Boston is depicted in this 1887 illustration. The workshop was actually just one of his boardinghouse rooms.

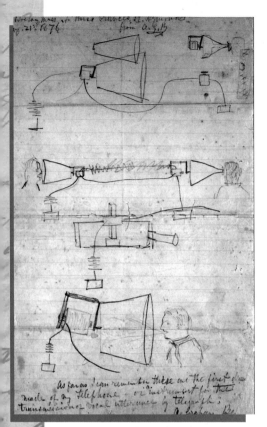

"The speaking telephone was born at that moment," wrote Watson. Before the long, hot night was over, Bell had sketched out a design for the first telephone.

Bell drew these sketches of his telephone design for a cousin in 1876. He wrote, "As far as I can remember these are the first drawings made of my telephone—or 'instrument for the transmission of vocal utterances by telegraph.'"

Backing Down and Gearing Up

The June accident proved to Alexander Graham Bell that his dream of the telephone was clearly within reach. But all was not rosy. Gardiner Greene Hubbard's ultimatum had infuriated Bell. Teaching the deaf to speak was his lifework—and Visible Speech was part of his family heritage! He wasn't going to give that up to invent a better telegraph—or even to please the father of the woman he loved.

Bell angrily wrote in a letter to Mabel's father that "If she does not come to love me well enough to accept me whatever my profession or business may be—I do not want her at all! I do not want a half-love, nor do I want her to marry my profession!" Mabel Hubbard herself put the conflict forever to rest on November 25, 1875. It was both her eighteenth birthday and

Thanksgiving the day she agreed to marry an astonished Alexander Graham Bell. He had won her heart! "I am afraid to go to sleep lest I should find it all a dream," Alexander wrote Mabel that night. "So I shall lie awake and think of you."

Gardiner Greene Hubbard had also backed down on pressuring Bell to put the harmonic telegraph before the telephone. The quest to invent a working telephone and get it patented was now in high gear, because Bell Patent Associates were worried about competition from Elisha Gray and other inventors. Bell had been experimenting in the attic above the electrical shop where Watson worked. But lots of inventors with wandering eyes came through that shop. So in January 1876 Bell moved into a new boardinghouse in Boston and made one of his rooms into a workshop. The telephone was coming along nicely! It had a mouthpiece with a membrane tightly stretched over one end, like the top of a drum. When Watson or Bell spoke into the mouthpiece, his voice created sound waves that set the membrane vibrating. The vibrations passed into a spring that vibrated over one end of an

Alexander Graham Bell and Mabel Hubbard enjoy a peaceful moment together in this c. 1880 photograph

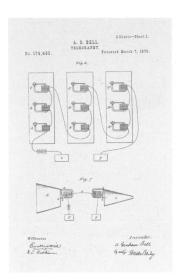

These drawings from a page in Bell's "Improvement in Telegraphy" patent carry its issuance date—March 7, 1876. The upper drawing (Fig. 6) shows the tuned reeds of a harmonic multiple telegraph. The lower drawing (Fig. 7) is a magneto-electric telephone.

electromagnet, creating an electrical current that reproduced the voice sounds. But the sounds were rough and garbled—no words could be understood.

It wasn't yet an invention you could box up and sell to the public. Still, the telephone's basic principles and design had been worked out. That winter, Alexander Graham Bell wrote up an explanation of his so-called magneto-electric telephone, along with labeled diagrams. The patent paperwork was filed on February 14, 1876—and not a moment too soon! Just a few hours later that same day, rival inventor Elisha Gray filed a **caveat**, warning

This photograph is of the magneto-electric prototype telephone Bell invented in 1875 and patented. This prototype could transmit recognizable sounds, but not clear speech.

Elisha Gray

Elisha Gray (1935–1901) was an American inventor based in Chicago who competed with Bell on the multiple telegraph and telautograph, as well as the telephone. In fact, Elisha Gray teamed up with the Western Union Telegraph Company against Bell in a court battle over the telephone's patent. Some consider Gray the true inventor of the telephone because the device he described in his patent caveat would have likely worked, while the magneto-electric telephone design in Bell's patent was somewhat different from the liquid transmitter model he went on to develop.

Gray made many telegraphic and electrical inventions and held about seventy patents. In 1872, he founded the Western Electric Manufacturing Company. He became a wealthy man and a respected professor of electricity at Oberlin College. But coming in second in the telephone race was understandably a lifelong sore point. After he died, a note he'd written was found that read, "The history of the telephone will never be fully written. . . . It is partly hidden away . . . and partly lying on the hearts and consciences of a few whose lips are sealed— some in death and others by a golden clasp whose grip is even tighter."

Though Bell is credited as being the inventor of the telephone, Elisha Gray also patented many similar inventions. In fact, some consider Gray to be the real inventor of the telephone.

other inventors that he would soon be filing a patent for a device to electrically transmit speech, claiming *he* was working on an "electric speaking telephone"! Luckily, Bell's detailed and thorough patent application got there first and was granted. Not a single person had yet spoken by telephone. But U.S. Patent No. 174,465 would become one of the most profitable inventions in history.

The First Telephone Message

Back from Washington, D.C., with a newly printed patent in hand, Alexander Graham Bell quickly got down to business. Now that his invention was protected by a patent, all that was left to do was make it work! On the first day back in the laboratory, Bell decided to try something different. He began experimenting with a new kind of transmitter—one that used liquid to help transfer voice vibrations into an electrical current. Watered-down battery acid seemed to make the sound loudest, he soon found.

Bell and Watson hooked it up and tried it out. When Watson spoke into the top of the transmitter box, his voice shook a membrane and an attached needle bobbed up and down in the liquid. The voice vibrations traveled from the transmitter to a wire that led to the receiver reed. "When Mr. Watson talked into the box an indistinct mumbling was heard at [the receiver]," Bell noted on March 9, 1876. The inventor could hear his assistant speaking, but the telephone's sound still wasn't clear enough to make out specific words.

The next morning, Thomas Watson made a new liquid transmitter. It looked a bit like a small tub with a speaking-tube mouthpiece coming out the top. Watson waited in Bell's bedroom with the telephone's reed receiver up against his ear. Bell was in a separate room with the new transmitter. "I then shouted into [the

Truth or Legend?

Why did Alexander Graham Bell speak those famous words, "Mr. Watson—Come here—I want to see you"? In Watson's account of the event, published in his autobiography, the tone of Bell's voice indicated that the inventor needed help, and when Watson rushed into Bell's room he saw that his mentor had spilled battery acid onto his clothes.

The acid-spilling-accident part of the first telephone call has become part of the legend of the event. However, it likely didn't happen. Bell made no mention of spilling acid in his account. He'd simply heard strange noises coming through the device and wanted to ask his assistant what he'd done. Watson's account wasn't published until he wrote his autobiography fifty years after the fateful day and long after Alexander Graham Bell had passed away. Perhaps Watson simply wanted to make the story as dramatic as he remembered feeling those many decades ago.

mouthpiece] the following sentence: 'Mr. Watson—Come here—I want to see you,'" Alexander Graham Bell wrote in his laboratory notebook.

A stunned twenty-two-year-old Thomas Watson rushed into the hallway where Bell was. "To my delight he came and declared that he had heard and understood what I said," wrote Bell. Alexander Graham Bell had transmitted the first words by telephone! The men switched places and Watson spoke the first telephoned words that Bell would hear: "Mr. Bell, do you understand what I say?"

Later, as the day's importance sunk in, Bell wrote a letter to his father: "Articulate speech was transmitted intelligibly this afternoon. I have constructed a new apparatus operated by the human voice. . . . This is a great day with me. I feel that I have at last struck the solution of a great problem—and the day is coming when telegraph wires will be laid on to houses just like water or gas—and friends converse with each other without leaving home." Alexander Graham Bell had invented the telephone. It was time to call the world and let them know.

On the fateful day when Alexander Graham Bell made the first telephone call to Thomas Watson—March 10, 1876—he wrote excitedly about his achievement to his father.

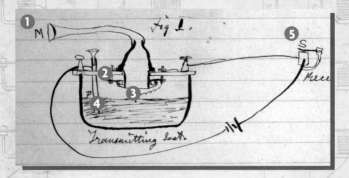

This sketch from a page of Alexander Graham Bell's personal notebook is dated March 10, 1876—the day of the first successful telephone call. It shows a sketch of the liquid transmitter and describes Bell's telephone call to Thomas Watson, but doesn't mention any spilled acid.

Bell's first telephone looked nothing like what you answer today. A person talked into an odd speaking tube over a tub of liquid that transmitted the voice vibrations into an electrical current. Here's how it worked:

1. Speaking into the transmitter's cone creates sound waves.
2. Sound waves vibrate the membrane stretched across the bottom of the cone.
3. The vibrations cause a metal needle in the center of the membrane to move up and down in a cup of watered-down acid.
4. When the needle moves closer to the bottom of the cup, more electricity is conducted to a wire there, and the current increases. The current weakens when the needle moves away from the wire at the bottom of the cup.
5. The changing, or undulating, current travels along a wire to the receiver. The receiver's metal reed vibrates with the undulating current, imitating speech sounds.

CHAPTER 7

Taking the Telephone on the Road

[W]hat a longing I have to see the places I remember so well—London, Bath, Edinburgh, and Elgin.

In 1876, the United States threw itself a hundredth birthday party, called the International **Centennial** Exhibition. Nearly ten million people came to Philadelphia to celebrate and see the exhibits of art, culture, foods, and the latest technological inventions. One odd-looking device sat in a small, out-of-the-way gallery within the exhibits representing Massachusetts. It was Alexander Graham Bell's new telephone.

As Bell readied his invention for the judges, no one watching would've guessed that the inventor was only twenty-nine. Bell had grown stout over the past year, and any hint of boyishness was long gone. He hadn't wanted to compete at the Centennial Exhibition. It was exam time back at Boston University. His students would need him—and he had tests to grade, too. But his fiancée,

At the 1876 Centennial Exhibition, Alexander Graham Bell demonstrated a telephone receiver (left) and transmitter (right). Shown are replicas of the originals from the Centennial Exposition.

This 1876 lithograph shows a panoramic view of the Centennial Exhibition buildings in Philadelphia's Fairmont Park. Millions of people from around the world attended the celebration and visited the exhibits.

Mabel Hubbard, talked him into going and showing off his invention. What wider audience was there than the biggest fair in American history?

One of the judges was the Centennial's most distinguished visitor: Dom Pedro, emperor of Brazil. On the hot afternoon of June 25, 1876, everyone stared as the emperor held the telephone receiver up to his ear. Meanwhile, five hundred feet away, Alexander Graham Bell began reciting Shakespeare into a transmitter. A startled Dom Pedro jumped out of his chair and exclaimed in astonishment, "I hear, I hear!" The other judges soon stampeded to be the next in line to listen to Bell's voice through the telephone. Loud cheers rose up after each successful test. The crowd around Bell's telephone made such a racket that exposition police thought the building was on fire! Famed English scientist Sir William Thomson declared it the most wonderful thing he'd seen in America: "Before long, friends will whisper their secrets over the electric wire."

Novelty or Necessity?

After several more months of hard work, Bell's telephone was much improved. It had evolved into a two-way speaking and listening device that could send and receive voice signals at distances of up to two miles over telegraph wires. However, though Bell's wonderful telephone set the judges on fire at the Centennial Exhibition, it wasn't making any money. President Rutherford B. Hayes summed up the attitude toward the telephone soon after when he said, "That's an amazing invention, but who would ever want to use one of them?"

The Bell Patent Association—now with four men instead of three (Thomas Sanders, Gardiner Greene Hubbard, Alexander Graham Bell, and

Dom Pedro (left), the emperor of Brazil, holds Alexander Graham Bell's (right) telephone receiver up to his ear as the inventor demonstrates his technology at the Centennial Exhibition.

Thomas Watson)—decided to try to make money by selling their telephone patents to Western Union. Who better to set up a telephone system than the company that already had a wire network strung across America? Bell's asking price was one hundred thousand dollars. The Western Union Telegraph Company's president declared Bell's telephone a mere toy and turned down the offer. It's considered one of the worst business decisions in American history. "Two years later those same patents could not have been bought for $25 million," wrote Watson. But in 1876, Western Union's rejection left the Bell Patent Association with an invention that hadn't made a penny—just as Gardiner Greene Hubbard had feared. They'd have to promote the telephone themselves.

This lithograph of the nineteenth president of the United States, Rutherford B. Hayes, was created in 1877, a year after he questioned the usefulness of the telephone.

The Western Union Telegraph Company's president declared Bell's telephone a mere toy and turned down the offer.

Perhaps remembering what demonstrations had done for Visible Speech, Bell soon arranged to demonstrate the telephone at public lectures. It was purely entertainment to most who came. Audiences were astonished when they heard Watson's voice coming through a box on a stage answering Bell's questions, even though he was city blocks away! The two men put on an entertaining show, adding drama and even singing. "I am the invisible Tom Watson!" the voice from the telephone would exclaim. "Everybody hears me! Nobody sees me!"

They were a hit.

The upper-class Hubbards were somewhat aghast that their daughter's fiancée was amusing audiences with such antics. But they couldn't complain about the results. Little more than a year after the Centennial Exhibition, nearly eight hundred Bell telephones had been installed. It was catching on as useful technology—not just an amusing novelty. In July 1877, Bell, Sanders, Watson, and Hubbard formed the Bell Telephone Company. With his invention finally making money, thirty-year-

This engraving illustrates a famous series of telephone demonstrations by Bell and Watson in 1877. Bell spoke from a lecture hall in Salem, Massachusetts, to Watson in Boston via telephone.

old Alexander Graham Bell could support a wife. Alexander and Mabel married on July 11, 1877. The inventor's wedding gift to Mabel was a thirty percent share of the Bell Telephone Company. It would make nineteen-year-old Mabel Bell a very wealthy woman.

Fit for a Queen and President

The newlyweds boarded a steamship in August and headed to Great Britain. "[W]hat a longing I have to see the places I remember so well—London, Bath, Edinburgh, and Elgin," Alexander Graham Bell wrote to his mother. When Alexander and Mabel arrived, he delighted in showing his bride all his old homes and haunts in England and Scotland. But the honeymoon trip to Britain soon turned into a working vacation. Inventor Alexander Graham Bell was becoming famous, and everyone in Britain wanted a see a demonstration of his amazing telephone—even the queen herself.

On January 14, 1878, Queen Victoria slowly entered the Council Room at Osborne House, along with her children—the duke of Connaught and Princess Beatrice. The fifty-eight-year-old monarch wore a black silk gown and widow's cap. After

This photograph of Alexander Graham Bell was taken on his honeymoon in July 1877. Alexander and Mabel were married at the Hubbard home and honeymooned at Niagara Falls before heading to Europe.

Ma Bell

The Bell Telephone Company formed by Bell, Watson, Hubbard, and Sanders in 1877 nearly failed. When Western Union Telegraph also entered the telephone business in 1877 using transmitters developed by Thomas Edison and Elisha Gray's receivers, the giant company quickly gobbled up much of the market. The Bell Company battled back by using improved transmitters and suing Western Union for illegally **infringing** on Bell's patents. In 1879, Western Union recognized Bell's patents and sold its telephone business to the Bell Company.

In 1885, the American Telephone and Telegraph Company (AT&T) was created to operate the long-distance network of the American Bell Telephone Company. AT&T eventually became the parent company of the Bell System, including AT&T and other telephone companies that supplied phone service to nearly every home and business in America. If you wanted telephone service, you had to get it from "Ma Bell." In 1974, the U.S. government sued AT&T, charging that it was an illegal monopoly. AT&T was broken up in 1984 into smaller regional "Baby Bell" companies, such as Southwestern Bell Corporation (SBC), and AT&T became a provider of long-distance service. Today AT&T Inc. is the largest telecommunications company in the United States. It provides data, video, and voice communications services to businesses, governments, and homes around the world.

receiving Her Majesty's invitation, Alexander Graham Bell had traveled to the royal residence on the Isle of Wight to set up the demonstrations. The queen sat and listened to telephone conversations from nearby buildings and the neighboring town, which was Cowes. At one point during the demonstration, Bell touched the queen's hand to offer her the telephone so she could listen in on a song. Onlookers were shocked by Bell's violation of royal rules. No one touches the queen! The error in etiquette didn't seem to dull Queen Victoria's excitement over the telephone. She wrote in her diary that night that it was "most extraordinary."

By the time Alexander Graham Bell left Europe almost a year later, much of the Continent knew of the telephone. But showing off his invention wasn't the only reason the Bells had stayed in Europe so long. Their daughter Elsie May was born on May 8, 1878, in London. By the time the couple arrived back in America, there were Bell telephones in hundreds of businesses and even a few private homes— including American author Mark Twain's residence. Even the U.S.

Years after Bell demonstrated his telephone for Queen Victoria, the queen reportedly recorded her voice on Bell's then new invention, the graphophone, in 1888. In this 1991 photograph, a museum curator holds up a fragile wax cylinder believed to contain the only known voice recording of Queen Victoria.

president who'd once wondered why anyone would want a telephone now called it "one of the greatest events since creation." The first White House telephone was installed in 1879, and President Hayes's first call was to Alexander Graham Bell.

Mabel Bell holds her daughter, Elsie May Bell. The Bells' firstborn child is three months old in this 1878 photograph. She was born in London, England.

CHAPTER 8

Onward as an Inventor

The inventor is a man who looks around upon the world and is not contented with things as they are.

The telephone made Alexander Graham Bell famous—and wealthy. But many imposter inventors and dishonest businessmen tried to cash in on the success of the "speaking telegraph." Bell summed it up in a letter to his wife, Mabel, in 1878: "The more fame a man gets for an invention, the more does he become a target for the world to shoot at."

The first to target the Bell Telephone Company was Western Union. The telegraph giant missed its chance to buy Bell's telephone patents—so instead tried to put Bell's company out of business. Western Union Telegraph Company teamed up with Elisha Gray and Thomas Edison. The two inventors came up with a telephone design that Western Union quickly began installing across the country. Western Union also made negative claims about Bell and his invention.

In this photograph c. 1887, Alexander Graham Bell and Thomas Watson examine a liquid transmitter similar to the one they used to make their first telephone call in 1876.

Newspapers printed stories calling Gray the true inventor of the telephone, and the competing inventors claimed that Bell couldn't have invented the device because he wasn't an electrician.

Bell Telephone was facing failure under the bullying of Western Union. So the Bell Telephone Company sued Western Union for illegally using its patent. Alexander Graham Bell and Thomas Watson testified in court, convincingly detailing how they'd invented the telephone. Smelling defeat, Western Union gave up. But it was only the first of a whopping six hundred court battles that the Bell Telephone Company would have to fight over two long decades. The total amount of paperwork caused by testimonies alone was over nine feet high! Happily, Alexander Graham Bell and his telephone patent won every legal case.

Western Union and other rivals tried to discredit Alexander Graham Bell by printing announcements claiming that Elisa Gray, not Bell, invented the telephone. The Bell Telephone Company often printed rebuttals, including this February 27, 1879, announcement.

"The inventor is a man who looks around upon the world and is not contented with things as they are," Alexander Graham Bell explained in a speech. "He wants to improve whatever he sees, he wants to benefit the world. . . ." Inventing technology and educating the deaf were the two things that he wanted to keep doing—not running Bell Telephone Company. So besides testifying in court, Bell didn't have much to do with the company that carried his name. And as he told his father-in-law, "business (which is hateful to me at all times) would fetter me [hold me back] as an inventor."

All the false legal claims against Alexander Graham Bell made him want to prove his worth as an inventor to the world. "I can't bear to hear that even friends should think that I stumbled upon an invention and that there is no more good in me," he wrote Mabel. He needn't have worried. Bell would go on to invent devices that record sound, aid the sick, and travel through the air and water. But he would never fully escape the shadow of his own fame as the inventor of the telephone.

This late 19th-century illustration shows a New York City street clogged with overhead telephone wires.

The Sound of Sunshine

Alexander Graham Bell said, "discoveries and inventions arise from the observation of little things." One such observation that Bell made was that America's streets were becoming a mess of crisscrossing telephone wires. He wondered: *Is there a way to transmit speech using beams of light instead of all those wires?* The answer to this question was an invention that Alexander Graham Bell considered to be greater than the telephone—the "wireless" photophone.

By late 1879, Alexander and Mabel were living in Washington, D.C. It was there that Bell started working on the photophone with a young man named Sumner Tainter. Together, they built their light-powered phone using mirrors, lenses, and an element that conducted electricity called selenium. Taken together, all these pieces completed a circuit from speaker to listener, like a telephone. But there were no wires involved.

After months of tinkering, Bell and Tainter had a working invention that could send voice messages hundreds of yards. Proud of his new invention, Bell poetically wrote his father: "I have heard articulate speech produced by sunlight! I have heard a ray of the sun laugh and cough and sing!" Alexander Graham Bell was so proud of his invention that he wanted to name their second child Photophone! Luckily for their daughter, Mabel talked him out of it. The Bells' second daughter was born February 15, 1880, and named Marian—but they called her Daisy.

Alexander Graham Bell imagined that the light-powered photophone would quickly replace the wire-bound telephone, allowing even ships at sea to communicate. But the photophone never became a practical device in Bell's lifetime. When Bell invented it, people still lit their homes with gas lamps and rode in horse-drawn carriages. They simply weren't ready for something as futuristic as the

This photograph of Bell's daughters was taken in 1880 or 1881. Big sister Elsie May is on the right and baby Marian (called Daisy) is on the left.

As depicted in this engraving, the photophone's receiver was a dish that concentrated the light onto a selenium crystal. The selenium created the sound-shaped electrical current that was converted back into sound that a person could hear.

Just like the telephone, Bell's photophone sent sound across distances. But instead of sending it along wires, the photophone used light. On a regular telephone, a magnet on a flexible membrane within a copper-wire circuit creates the speech-sending undulating electrical current. Bell's photophone instead used light-sensitive selenium and a beam of sunlight to connect a transmitter to a receiver. Selenium is a photoelectric element. Its resistance, or ability to conduct electricity, is changed when light shines on it.

photophone. Still, it wasn't a complete loss. The photophone demonstrated principles that were later developed into fiber optics and wireless mobile phones. It would take nearly a century, however, for technology—and the public—to catch up to the imagination of Alexander Graham Bell.

Tragedy and Inspiration

Imagination and observation weren't the only sources of Alexander Graham Bell's inspiration. Unfortunately, so was tragedy. And it was the American tragedy of a president who lay dying from a bullet wound that inspired Bell to invent the telephonic probe. The year was 1881, and President James

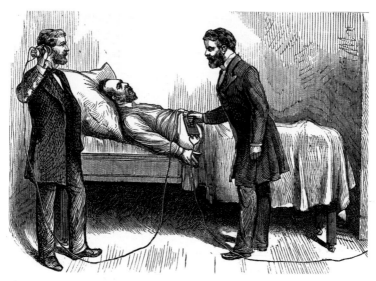

This undated engraving depicts Alexander Graham Bell (right) attempting to find the bullet lodged in the infection-ridden body of President Garfield using his newly invented metal detector in July 1881.

Garfield—who had been in office for only a few months—was shot by a mentally ill man named Charles Guiteau at a Washington, D.C., train station.

Garfield survived the shooting, but one of the bullets went deep into his body. In 1881, there were no X-rays, nor any understanding that germs are the cause of infections. Doctors crudely tried to find the bullet by poking unwashed fingers and unsterilized instruments into Garfield's wound. The president's body soon raged with infection, and the bullet remained lodged. "The whole world watched," Bell remembered. "And hopes and fears filled every passing hour. No one could venture to predict the end so long as the position of the bullet remained unknown."

Alexander Graham Bell went to Washington to try to find the

bullet with his latest invention, the metal detector. It was simply a telephone receiver hooked up to an electromagnet. When the device passed something metallic—in this case, a bullet—the tone coming through the receiver would change. The inventor had successfully tested it by searching for bullets that had been shot into slabs of meat. But Alexander Graham Bell's device was unable to locate the bullet inside President Garfield. Eighty miserable days after being shot, Garfield died. Ironically, if he had been left to recover on his own, and not been poked and prodded, Garfield probably would have pulled through.

Bell channeled his grief into work, inventing a device to aid people having trouble breathing.

Why did the metal detector miss Garfield's bullet? The most widely accepted theory is that the metal from the bedsprings Garfield lay on interfered with the readings. But luckily, the device was later successfully used to find bullets in other patients.

Bell also went on to invent a similar bullet detector called the telephonic probe. It saved the lives of many gunshot victims and soldiers before X-ray machines. "Certainly no man can have a higher incentive than the hope of relieving suffering and saving life," Alexander Graham Bell humbly remarked. Unfortunately, it would be his own family's suffering that would soon become his next incentive to invent.

While President Garfield lay dying, Mabel Bell was in labor with her third child. The Bells were summering in Massachusetts, but Alexander was in Washington working on his bullet detector. Mabel gave birth to a baby boy on August 15, 1881. But baby Edward was premature and died from breathing difficulties within a few hours. Bell channeled his grief into work, inventing a device to aid people having trouble breathing. Alexander called the world's first artificial **respirator** a vacuum jacket. The invention was an iron cylinder that snugly wrapped around a patient's chest, with a hand pump that changed the air pressure inside the metal cylinder. This squeezed and released the patient's chest,

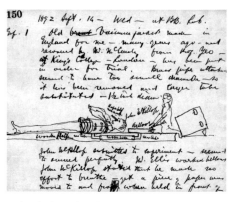

A sketch drawn by Alexander Graham Bell illustrates his 1892 notes on his vacuum jacket design, the first artificial respirator.

mechanically forcing air in and out of the lungs. In later years, the vacuum jacket would evolve into the iron lung, a breathing machine used for polio victims.

Unfortunately, no new invention could save Mabel and Alexander's last child. Robert Bell was also born prematurely on November 17, 1883. "Poor little one," Mabel wrote. "It was so pretty and struggled so hard to live, opened his eyes once or twice to the world and then passed away." Alexander and Mabel would have no more children.

The year 1883 didn't pass without some happy events for Alexander Graham Bell. He had long dreamed of opening a new kind of school for deaf children—one where entire classrooms of deaf kids learned to speak using the Visible Speech system. After years of planning and training a teacher, the school finally opened in 1883. That fall, deaf children began attending a Washington, D.C., school in a brick building surrounded by gardens. "Mr. Bell's" school was open for business.

CHAPTER 9

A Life's Work

[R]ecognition of my work for and interest in the education of the deaf has always been more pleasing to me than even recognition of my work with the telephone.

The sounds of recess filled the air around the old-fashioned building in Washington, D.C., as young boys and girls played in the two-story school's garden and lawn. A closer look revealed that half a dozen of the children were deaf. But the children who couldn't hear played with the hearing kids, reading lips and speaking as best they could. When recess was over, the hearing students—all kindergartners—shuffled into the downstairs classroom. Elsie and Daisy Bell were two of the kindergartners who attended their father's school. The six deaf students climbed the stairs to their second-floor room of Mr. Bell's school.

This 1885 family portrait photograph shows, from right to left: Alexander Graham Bell, daughter Daisy, wife Mabel, and daughter Elsie.

The teachers and students of Mr. Bell's school in Washington, D.C., posed for this 1883 photograph. It was a very progressive school for its time: deaf and hearing children shared a play yard.

The upstairs room wasn't like most classrooms in 1883. The students shared a low table instead of being separated in bolted down desks. It was filled with pictures, games, toys, and a soft floor rug—things that appealed to their working senses of sight and touch. Many objects around the room were labeled in both English and in Visible Speech. A young woman taught the students at the day school opened by Alexander Graham Bell that fall. She helped them learn to lip-read by reading the names on the labels. And the Visible Speech symbols helped the students learn to speak.

Opening the Washington, D.C., school had been a dream of Bell's for many years. He had never lost interest in deaf education, what he called "my life-work." Even while honeymooning and demonstrating the telephone to Queen Victoria in 1878, Bell found time to open another school for the deaf in Greenock, Scotland. He wrote Mabel from Scotland, "I have been so happy in my little school, happier than at any time since the telephone took my mind away from this work."

But telephone work would again take Bell's mind away from educating the deaf. The constant court battles over the telephone's patents kept him from being able to run the Washington school. Mr. Bell's school sadly closed after two short—though successful—years. He wrote that the school's failure was the most disappointing experience of his life.

The Deaf-Education Debate

Alexander Graham Bell wasn't a man to let disappointment hold him back for long. And he would continue to do everything he could to help break down the barriers between the deaf and the hearing. Bell knew firsthand how most deaf people were cut off from society. His mother was deaf, his wife was deaf, and he had personal relationships with many of his deaf students and their families. "Who can picture the isolation of their lives?" Bell passionately asked in a speech about the lives of the deaf. "[Imagine] the solitude of an intellectual being in the midst of a crowd of happy beings with whom he can not communicate and who can not communicate with him. . . . The sense of loneliness in the midst of so many is oppressive."

Bell knew firsthand how most deaf people were cut off from society.

During Bell's time, many deaf children didn't go to school at all. Few places had public schools for the deaf, and private schools were too expensive for most parents. Deaf children were often considered "slow" and were forced to communicate with gestures and grunts that most people couldn't understand. Those who did get an education were usually sent away to boarding schools. But Bell believed that regular day schools were better for deaf children, since he thought that children living at home with their families would be more motivated to learn to speak and lip-read.

Alexander Graham Bell believed that deaf children should be taught to speak and read lips so they could live more independent lives—just as his wife, Mabel, had done. But his strong beliefs were challenged by another pioneer of deaf education, Edward Gallaudet.

Gallaudet was the youngest son of Thomas Hopkins Gallaudet, the founder of America's first school for the deaf. Like Alexander Graham Bell, Edward Gallaudet had a mother who was deaf. But unlike Bell, Gallaudet believed that the deaf should not be made to speak—that instead sign language was the most practical and rewarding form of communication for the deaf community. It was an argument that boiled down to "oralism versus manualism," or "speech versus gesture."

To help promote his ideas about educating the deaf, Bell founded the American Association to Promote the Teaching of Speech to the Deaf. When the association was started in 1890, only about forty percent of deaf students learned to speak as part of their education. Thirty years later, that percentage had doubled. The organization was eventually

Edward Gallaudet, shown in this photograph taken between 1870 and 1880, was a deaf-education pioneer who advocated manualism, or sign language, over teaching the deaf to speak.

renamed the Alexander Graham Bell Association for the Deaf and Hard of Hearing, in honor of its founder. Today it remains an organization dedicated to "advocating independence through listening and talking."

Alexander Graham Bell worked to promote deaf education in the United States and abroad for his entire life. He donated nearly half a million dollars to charities and schools for the deaf. Bell also invented the audiometer, a device to measure how well a person can hear. He used his audiometer to test the hearing of hundreds of people. Many were children who'd been labeled as lazy, but were actually struggling in school because they couldn't hear well.

"Bell was never happier than when he was holding a deaf

Edward Gallaudet was president of the Columbia Institution for the Instruction of the Deaf and Dumb (now Gallaudet University) in Washington, D.C., for 53 years. This 1962 photograph shows a girl learning to speak sign language at Gallaudet.

The Audiometer

The audiometer combined Alexander Graham Bell's two great passions—inventing and helping the hearing-impaired. Bell invented the audiometer in 1879 and presented it to the National Academy of Sciences in 1885. It worked by creating an electrical current in a wire coil connected in circuit to a telephone receiver. Test subjects held the receiver up their ears and listened as the loudness of the sound was varied. The unit used to measure the relative loudness of sounds, the bel or decibel, is named for Alexander Graham Bell.

A boy is taking a hearing test with an audiometer in this photograph. The machine produces simple vibrations of various tones at different volumes to measure hearing and detect hearing loss.

child in his arms," a family friend commented. And Alexander Graham Bell was never too busy to help find a way to educate a deaf child. He'd created a glove with letters of the alphabet written on the fingers to teach five-year-old Georgie Sanders to finger-spell words back in Boston. And Bell would arrange for a miracle-working instructor to tutor a young deaf and blind girl named Helen Keller.

A Door Through Darkness

Captain Arthur H. Keller was no stranger to war—or defeat. He'd been an officer in the Confederate army in the U.S. Civil War. Now Keller and his wife, Kate, were losing a battle with their own child. Little Helen Keller was both blind and deaf. An illness had taken her sight and hearing as a baby, and, like many other deaf children, Helen therefore could not speak. Now six years old, she had grown into a wild, angry child—kicking, scratching, and choking out screams to try to get what she wanted. What would become of Helen? Many like her ended up living in horrific institutions with the insane. But Captain and Kate Keller were told that a famous man and educator of the deaf might be able to help their daughter. The Kellers decided to take Helen to meet Alexander Graham Bell.

Helen liked taking trips. She couldn't see the scenery or hear the city sounds. But the jostling feeling of trains and horse carriages was exciting. It was a long trip from Helen's Tuscumbia, Alabama, home to Washington, D.C., in 1887. Once at Bell's home, Helen climbed up and sat on the knee of this large man her parents had brought her to meet. Bell placed his watch in Helen's hand and made it chime, which he knew Helen would be able to feel. Bell immediately understood the crude signs and gestures she used to try to communicate. He saw intelligence and an admirable spirit in this little girl completely isolated inside herself. Helen felt Bell's tender sympathy and understanding of her world. Helen Keller

Helen Keller (left) and her teacher Anne Sullivan (right) posed for this photograph in 1893. Keller's books and the play *The Miracle Worker* made the pair world-famous celebrities.

and Alexander Graham Bell became friends at once.

Bell told the Kellers that he thought Helen could be taught to communicate—given the right teacher. He recommended contacting Perkins School for the Blind in Boston to help find the right tutor. Helen would later write of meeting Bell: "[T]hat interview would be the door through which I should pass from darkness into light." The name of the twenty-year-old tutor who came to the Keller home was Anne Sullivan. Within a month, Helen understood that the words Anne was spelling out into her hand were names for the things around her. It was this breakthrough that allowed Helen to finally communicate with the world.

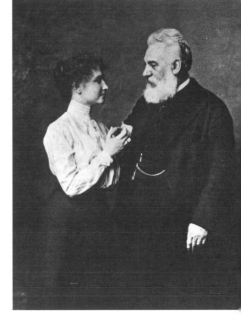

Helen Keller speaks her thoughts into Alexander Graham Bell's hand using a manual alphabet in this c. 1901 photograph.

Soon young Helen and Anne Sullivan could "talk" by finger spelling. Then Helen learned to read and write by feeling raised letters with the braille alphabet. "Dear Mr. Bell," Helen wrote at age eight. "I am glad to write you a letter. . . . I can read stories in my book. I can write and spell and count. . . ." Helen knew that most people spoke with their mouths, not with sign language or by finger spelling. She learned to read lips by placing her fingers on the lips and throat of the speaker. Helen could sense the vibrations when words were spoken and could feel the shape of the mouth. Amazingly, Helen was able to use this skill to learn to speak around age ten.

Helen Keller

Thanks to her teacher Anne Sullivan (1866–1936), blind and deaf Helen Keller (1880–1968) eventually learned to communicate with the outside world. Keller helped to found the Massachusetts Commission for the Blind and raised more money for the American Foundation for the Blind than any other person. Helen Keller went to college and became an author. She wrote several books, including *The Story of My Life* (1902). *The Miracle Worker* is a play and movie that dramatizes Keller's childhood.

By the time of this c. 1914 photograph, Helen Keller had graduated from college and was a famous author and lecturer.

A Lifelong Friendship

Alexander Graham Bell closely followed Helen's progress. Helen Keller was living proof that the deaf and deaf-blind could learn to communicate with innovative teaching. Bell was grateful for the public attention that Helen's life brought to deaf education. And while many called Anne Sullivan a "miracle worker," Bell knew better. It was Sullivan's unique teaching methods that had broken through Helen's isolation. Bell believed they were methods others could benefit from, too.

Helen Keller finally connected the water that was running over her with the letters *W-A-T-E-R* that her teacher spelled into her hand. Anne Sullivan "spoke" to Helen as they explored the garden and house, just as you would with a hearing child learning to talk. Sullivan didn't always stop to explain new words. She let Helen figure out what they meant through **context**, as a hearing child does. Bell believed that these and other teaching methods that Sullivan used could benefit many deaf and deaf-blind children.

Helen Keller and Alexander Graham Bell became lifelong friends. In 1893, he traveled with Helen and Anne Sullivan to Niagara Falls, on the border between the United States and Canada. Standing near the falls, Bell gave Helen a feather pillow. She held the pillow against her chest, and it magnified the vibrations she felt from the powerful falling water. "You can never imagine how I felt when I stood in the presence of Niagara until you have the same mysterious sensations yourself," Helen wrote her mother. "I could hardly realize that it was water that I felt rushing and plunging with impetuous fury at my feet. It seemed as if it were some living thing rushing on to some terrible fate. . . . I had the same feeling once before when I first stood by the great ocean and felt its waves beating against the shore. I suppose you feel so, too, when you gaze up to the stars in the stillness of the night, do you not?"

For Dr. Bell. With dearest Love From the Author

AUTUMN.

Oh, what a glory doth the world put on
These peerless, perfect autumn days
There is a beautiful spirit of gladness everywhere.
The wooded waysides are luminous with brightly painted leaves;
The forest-trees with royal grace have donned
Their gorgeous autumn tapestries;
And even the rocks and fences are broidered
With ferns, sumachs and brilliantly tinted ivies.
But so exquisitely blended are the lights and shades,
The golds, scarlets and purples, that no sense is wearied;
For God himself hath painted the landscape.

The hillsides gleam with golden corn;
Apple and peach-trees bend beneath their burdens of golden fruit.
The golden-rods, too, are here, whole armies of them,
With waving plumes, resplendent with gold;
And about the wild grapes, purple and fair and full of sunshine,
The little birds southward going
Linger, like travellers at an Inn,
And sip the perfumed wine.
And far away the mountains against the blue sky stand
Calm and mysterious, like prophets of God,
Wrapped in purple mist.

But now a change o'er the bright and glorious sky has come
The threatening clouds stand still,
The silent skies are dark and solemn;
The mists of morning hide the golden face of day.
And a mysterious hand has stripped the trees;
And with rustle and whir the leaves descend,
And like little frightened birds
Lie trembling on the ground.
Bare and sad the forest-monarchs stand
Like kings of eld, all their splendor swept away.

And down from his ice-bound realm in the North
Comes Winter, with snowy locks, and tear-drops frozen on his cheeks;
For he is the brother of Death, and acquainted with Sorrow.
Autumn sees him from afar,
And, as a child to her father runneth,
She to the protecting arms of kindly Winter fleeth;
And in his mantle of snow
Tenderly he folds her lovely form,
And on his breast she falls asleep
Ere yet the storm-winds have loosed their fury
Upon a white and silent world.

She sleeps unconscious of the sorrow that must be,
And dreams perchance of sylvan music,
And the splendor that was, and will again be hers;
For Autumn dies not 'Tis as the Poet says:
"There is no Death. What seems so is transition."
All that is divine lives
In some nobler sphere, some fairer form.

Helen Keller.

Hulton, Penn., Oct 27th, 1893.

Thirteen-year-old Helen Keller dedicated this poem she wrote, "For Dr. Bell, With dearest Love, From the Author." The poem, titled "Autumn," is dated October 27, 1893.

These are amazing observations for a not quite thirteen-year-old girl who couldn't see or hear what she was describing. When Helen Keller and Alexander Graham Bell were together, they were constantly finger spelling back and forth. Bell taught her about science and his work. "He makes you feel that if you only had a little more time, you, too, might be an inventor," Helen wrote. Bell helped pay for Helen to attend college, and she was a guest at the Bells' home on many occasions throughout her life. When Helen Keller wrote her autobiography, she dedicated it, "To Alexander Graham Bell. Who has taught the deaf to speak and enabled the listening ear to hear speech from the Atlantic to the Rockies, I dedicate this *Story of My Life*."

"To Alexander Graham Bell. Who has taught the deaf to speak and enabled the listening ear to hear speech from the Atlantic to the Rockies, I dedicate this Story of My Life.*"*

Helen Keller understood that educating the deaf was Alexander Graham Bell's lifework. Bell once said, "One would think I had never done anything worthwhile but the telephone. That is because it is a money-making invention. It is a pity so many people make money the **criterion** of success. I wish my experiences had resulted in enabling the deaf to speak with less difficulty. That would have made me truly happy." At age seventy, he wrote that "recognition of my work for and interest in the education of the deaf has always been more pleasing to me than even recognition of my work with the telephone."

CHAPTER 10

Spreading Science

In scientific researches, there are no unsuccessful experiments; every experiment contains a lesson.

Three men crowded around a small machine one early-autumn day in 1881. The men had been working on improving an invention that could record sounds and play them back—a phonograph. They'd been tinkering with their machine for months in the Washington, D.C., Volta Laboratory. The men hoped that the contraption could finally play back a clear-sounding recording. Now it was time to test it. The device was switched on, and out came a perfectly understandable

The graphophone pictured in this undated photograph was developed by Bell's Volta Laboratory and patented in 1886. It recorded sound on a wax cylinder.

BELL-TAINTER MACHINE
ENTERED IN CATALOGUE AT THE
NATIONAL MUSEUM, NOV. 30, 1920
MUSEUM CATALOGUE NO. 287653.

This engraving shows two men listening to recorded sounds on a graphophone. Sumner Tainter and Chichester Bell later developed the graphophone into a dictating machine and started the Dictaphone Company.

sentence: "I am a graphophone, and my mother was a phonograph." It worked! The three men—Sumner Tainter, Chichester Bell, and Alexander Graham Bell—congratulated one another.

Thomas Edison had invented the phonograph four years earlier. But Edison's phonograph didn't work very well. One scientist called Edison's device "the most marvelous and useless invention ever made." Edison soon gave up on it, believing it would never make money. Alexander Graham Bell disagreed, and he decided to turn

Thomas Edison is shown in this c. 1877 photograph slouching in a chair listening to his favorite invention—the phonograph.

The Phonograph

Thomas Edison invented the phonograph in 1877. His invention used a tinfoil-covered cylinder shaped like a can to record and play back sound. Attached to the cylinder was a needle connected to a vibrating diaphragm. A hand crank spun the cylinder. When a person spoke into a mouthpiece, it produced sound waves that made the diaphragm and needle vibrate and carve dents into the spinning cylinder's tinfoil. Listeners played back recorded sounds using a different needle, also attached to a diaphragm set against the cylinder.

The needle rode up and down over the dents on the spinning cylinder, making the needle and diaphragm vibrate and reproducing the recorded sounds. But Edison's original phonograph didn't sound very good, and the tinfoil indentations were ruined after a few playings.

The Volta Laboratory's Chichester Bell, Sumner Tainter, and Alexander Graham Bell improved on Edison's invention in many ways. They quickly found that a wax-covered cylinder lasted longer than a tinfoil one. The needle cut a permanent groove into the wax instead of just making flimsy dents in tinfoil. And they eventually patented the first flat, round, hard wax disks—records!—for recording sounds. The Volta team also invented a flexible zigzagging needle instead of a stiff one that rode up and down. This greatly improved the quality of the phonograph's sound.

This c. 1901 advertisement for the Edison Triumph model phonograph uses Uncle Sam as a patriotic spokesman for the American invention. Its price—$50—was a lot of money a hundred years ago, more than a thousand of today's dollars.

Edison's crude invention into a practical machine that recorded sounds and played them back. Not only would a better-working phonograph allow people to record and listen to music and speeches, but it also gave Bell a chance to beat Edison at his own game. Edison had invented a carbon transmitter for Western Union that had improved on Bell's telephone design. Now Bell had improved an invention of Edison's! An irritated Edison ended up having to buy the rights to Bell's improved phonograph patent so he could turn his own invention into a profitable product.

> *Alexander Graham Bell . . . decided to turn Edison's crude invention into a practical machine that recorded sounds and played them back.*

Alexander Graham Bell, shown here in 1877, greatly improved upon Thomas Edison's original phonograph.

Scientific Investments

In 1880, Alexander Graham Bell was awarded the $10,000 Volta Prize by the French government for his invention of the telephone. Bell named the Volta Laboratory for the scientific award whose prize money funded it. He hired electrician Sumner Tainter and his chemist cousin, Chichester Bell, to work at the lab near the Bells' Washington, D.C., home. Bell's work with Thomas Watson had taught him the value of scientific teamwork. And Bell backed that belief with money. "In scientific researches, there are no unsuccessful experiments; every experiment contains a lesson," he wrote. "If we don't get the results anticipated and stop right there, it is the man that is unsuccessful, not the experiment."

Bell also understood how important communication was in science. The inventor decided to help scientists keep up with new scientific discoveries and findings by rescuing a failing magazine called *Science*. Thomas Edison had funded the magazine's start-up in 1880, but he stopped supporting it when it failed to make money. So Alexander Graham Bell and his father-in-law, Gardiner Greene Hubbard, took over the magazine and kept it alive.

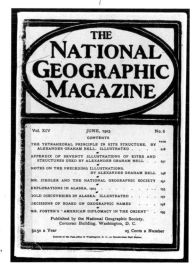

Vol. XIV   JUNE, 1903   No. 6

CONTENTS

THE TETRAHEDRAL PRINCIPLE IN KITE STRUCTURE. BY
  ALEXANDER GRAHAM BELL. ILLUSTRATED 218

APPENDIX OF SEVENTY ILLUSTRATIONS OF KITES AND
  STRUCTURES USED BY ALEXANDER GRAHAM BELL . . 231

NOTES ON THE PRECEDING ILLUSTRATIONS.
           BY ALEXANDER GRAHAM BELL . 248

MR. ZIEGLER AND THE NATIONAL GEOGRAPHIC SOCIETY . 251

EXPLORATIONS IN ALASKA, 1903 255

GOLD DISCOVERIES IN ALASKA. ILLUSTRATED 257

DECISIONS OF BOARD ON GEOGRAPHIC NAMES 258

MR. FOSTER'S "AMERICAN DIPLOMACY IN THE ORIENT" . 259

Published by the National Geographic Society,
Corcoran Building, Washington, D. C.

$2.50 a Year   25 Cents a Number

Entered at the Post-office in Washington, D. C., as Second-class Mail Matter.

Alexander Graham Bell not only helped found *The National Geographic Magazine*, but also wrote articles for it. His piece, "The Tetrahedral Principle in Kite Structure," is in this June 1903 issue.

The magazine has been published ever since, and today *Science* is one of the most important scientific journals in the world. Bell and Hubbard also went on to start another magazine—one called *The National Geographic Magazine*.

The World and All That's in It

Alexander Graham Bell wanted everyone—not just scientists—to better understand their world. To help in that goal, Bell and his father-in-law helped set up the National Geographic Society in 1888. Bell took part in shaping *The National Geographic Magazine* into one that was packed full of dazzling photographs, illustrations, and maps. "The world and all that is in it is our theme," he announced, and he eventually became president of the society in 1899.

The young man who took on the day-to-day job of heading the magazine was Gilbert Grosvenor. Bell advised the young editor to show the world as it was. This meant including photographs of people in their traditional dress—even if that meant they were mostly undressed.

Grosvenor successfully guided *The National Geographic Magazine* for more than half a century. And Gilbert Grosvenor also became part of the family. He and Bell's daughter Elsie were married in 1900. In 1905, younger daughter Daisy Bell also married a man she met through the society, a botanist named David Fairchild. Alexander Graham Bell would eventually have ten grandchildren!

Opposite: Elsie May Bell (left), her young son Melville Bell, and her husband, Gilbert Grosvenor, posed for this photograph in 1902. Elsie and Gilbert Grosvenor eventually had seven children, two sons and five daughters.

With the magazine in good hands, Bell felt it was time to move on. He stepped down as president of the society and devoted his time to his other interests, as well as to his family. He found a place where he could do all these things, far from the pressures and summer heat of Washington, D.C. Beinn Bhreagh (pronounced *ban vreeah*), which means "beautiful mountain" in **Gaelic**, was calling.

CHAPTER 11

Into the Air

If a kite flies well . . . when loaded with the equivalent to a man and motor, then if provided with an engine, it should travel through the air. . . .

The year was 1885, and newspaper editor Arthur McCurdy was getting frustrated with his newfangled telephone. He was desperately trying to call his brother, but the call wasn't getting through. And there wasn't any telephone repair service in the remote Canadian province of Nova Scotia, where McCurdy lived. But as the newspaperman fought with his phone, he noticed a tall gentleman peering at him through the office window. The distinguished-looking stranger entered the office and asked, "Your telephone won't talk back to you?" After McCurdy explained the problem, the gentleman screwed off the mouthpiece, fiddled with the transmitter, and put it back together. Miraculously, the telephone worked fine. When a grateful McCurdy asked the stranger how he knew how to fix a telephone, the man smiled. "My name is Alexander Graham Bell," he said.

Lucky for Arthur McCurdy, the Bells had been in Nova Scotia on vacation. But Mabel and Alexander fell in love with one of its little towns—called Baddeck—and were coming up with fewer and fewer reasons to leave. The land, climate, and people reminded Bell of his Scottish homeland, a feeling many must have shared before him, since the name *Nova Scotia* means "New

The Bell family built an estate in Baddeck, Nova Scotia and spent much of their time there. In this 1890 photograph, Alexander Graham Bell (bottom row, second from right) spends time with his family and friends in Baddeck.

Scotland." Eventually, the Bells opted to stay, cementing their commitment to the area by building an enormous estate they called Beinn Bhreagh, overlooking the sea. "The children are delighted with their free, wild life here," wrote Mabel.

Alexander Graham Bell had become a U.S. citizen in 1882, but he loved Canada and spent much of his life there. "Though I cannot claim to be a Canadian," he once said, "I have a warm spot in my heart for Canada." Beinn Bhreagh wasn't just a summer vacation spot for the Bells. Over the next thirty-six years, they would live in both Washington, D.C. and Canada. At Beinn Bhreagh, Bell built laboratories and continued his work; the lack of obligations, the wide-open spaces, and the brisk seaside winds were perfect for the last great idea Bell had up his sleeve. It was one he'd dreamed about since boyhood—a flying machine.

Uplifting Experiments

Many early experimenters in human flight paid a high price. Not all the "birdmen" who strapped on giant wings, harnessed themselves into hang gliders, or climbed into smoke-spewing flying contraptions lived to tell about it! Alexander Graham Bell wisely started his study of human flight from the safety of the ground. "I have been continuously at work upon experiments relating to kites," he wrote, ". . . because of the intimate connection of the subject with the flying machine problem." His plan was to design a kite that could safely lift a person; once that was perfected, he would then add an engine to it. "If a kite flies well . . . when loaded with the equivalent to a man and motor, then if provided with an engine, it should travel through the air . . . ," he wrote. It was the same plan that two bicycle-making brothers named Wright were using, too.

Soon kites of all sizes and shapes soared above Beinn Bhreagh. Some of the locals thought their famous neighbor was crazy to spend his days flying kites. "He goes up there on the side of the hill on sunny afternoons and with a lot of thing-ma-jigs, fools away the whole blessed day, flying kites, mind you," remarked local boatman John Hamilton Parkin. "He sets up a blackboard and puts down figures about these kites and queer machines he keeps bobbing around in the sky. Dozens of them he has. . . . It's the greatest foolishness I ever did see."

Even Helen Keller thought her friend a bit obsessed after a visit in 1901. "Mr. Bell has nothing but kites and flying-machines on his tongue's end," she wrote. But the "hobby" was a thrill for the young deaf-blind woman. One day, Keller told Bell that the

Bell (far right) and his assistants experiment with a giant ring-shaped kite in this 1908 photograph.

strings he would be using for a particular large kite seemed too weak. Bell didn't agree and sent the kite up anyway. "It began to pull and tug, and lo, the wires broke, and off went the [kite]," wrote Keller. "After that he asked me if the strings were all right and changed them at once when I answered in the negative. Altogether we had great fun."

Triangle Power

The skies above Bell's kite field were filled with box kites covered in red silk, white ring-shaped kites, cylindrical spool kites, and even star-shaped kites. But Bell soon found his favorite kite shape—a tetrahedron. A tetrahedron is a four-sided object whose sides and base are all triangles. Its design

Alexander Graham Bell's triangular design can be seen in this 1906 tetrahedron kite.

made for a particularly light kite, but one that was very strong. "I believe [the tetrahedron] will prove of importance not only in kite architecture," he wrote, "but in forming all sorts of skeleton frameworks for all sorts of constructing." Tetrahedral arches and supports would also work for bridges and heavy ceilings, Bell reasoned.

Bell put his beloved tetrahedron to work in kite construction. In 1905, he assembled thirteen hundred silk-covered wood tetrahedral cells into a massive kite called the *Frost King*. The kite looked like a flying piece of giant honeycomb. One worker was unexpectedly lifted forty feet into the air when he held on to the *Frost King* too long! But the "accident" proved that Bell's tetrahedral kite design had the power to carry humans into the air. Could it also carry an engine and be steered? Could Bell's designs be made into a flying machine?

The Wright Brothers

The *Wright Flyer* is shown in this 1903 photograph on the sands of Kill Devil Hill in Kitty Hawk, North Carolina, three days before it made the first flight by a powered, heavier-than-air flying machine—an airplane.

Wilbur Wright (1867–1912) and Orville Wright (1871–1948) were brothers and bicycle makers from Ohio who experimented with kites and human-controlled gliders. After developing propellers and an engine, they achieved the first powered, sustained, and controlled airplane flight in their *Wright Flyer* on December 17, 1903, near Kitty Hawk, North Carolina. In 1905, they built and flew the first fully practical airplane, which could turn, circle, and fly for more than half an hour.

Aerial Experiments

By the time the *Frost King* flew, the race to build the first flying machine was already won. Orville and Wilbur Wright flew the world's first airplane in 1903. And by 1905, the Wrights had an airplane that could stay in the air for more than thirty minutes. But aeronautics was a young science with lots of room for improvement. Bell believed that aerodromes ("air runner" in Greek), as he called airplanes, needed to be safer. How? Besides experimenting with ways to make airplanes more stable, Bell wanted to design an aerodrome that could glide back down to earth and safely land even if its engine suddenly died.

Besides enthusiasm, one of the most important factors in getting a new project off the ground is money. Mabel Bell

This 1908 photograph shows some members of the Aerial Experiment Association (AEA). From left to right are Casey Baldwin, Thomas Selfridge, Glenn Curtiss, Alexander Graham Bell, and Douglas McCurdy. On the far right is the secretary of the Aero Club of America, Augustus Post.

proposed that her husband form an organization to more easily get the funding he needed. And so the Aerial Experiment Association (AEA) was born in 1907. It included engineers Casey Baldwin and Douglas McCurdy (son of the newspaperman with the faulty phone), motorcycle racer and engine builder Glenn Hammond Curtiss, and U.S. Army lieutenant Thomas Selfridge. Mabel Bell personally funded the AEA, becoming the first woman to give money to a research organization.

The AEA's first project was getting one of Bell's kites into the air—with a person on it. The *Cygnet* was Bell's biggest kite ever. It was made up of more than thirty-three hundred red silk tetrahedral cells and was attached to floating pontoons that were connected by rope to a boat. On December 6, 1907, Selfridge lay

Alexander Graham Bell stands to the right as his enormous kite, the *Cygnet*, is taken out of its shed onto a dock on Great Bras d'Or Lake in this 1907 photograph.

down inside a flat section of the huge kite. The boat pulled the *Cygnet* over Great Bras d'Or Lake, and the kite rose 104 feet into the air. Selfridge hovered steadily overhead in the kite for seven long minutes. When the wind died down, the *Cygnet* gracefully descended toward the water. Selfridge (or someone on the boat) was supposed to cut the rope connecting the kite and boat as soon as the *Cygnet* set down. But Selfridge couldn't see out of the kite very well, and a puff of smoke from the boat's engine clouded the view. No one saw the kite's pontoons hit the water, so the rope wasn't cut in time. The speeding boat instantly jerked the delicate kite forward, dragging it through the lake and ripping it to pieces. Selfridge had to be rescued from the freezing water.

Selfridge had to be rescued from the freezing water.

The AEA decided it was time to try a two-stacked-wings "biplane" design—like the one that was working for the Wrights. Selfridge designed the *Red Wing* complete with an engine. Baldwin piloted the red-silk-covered airplane on a short hundred-yard flight, but it tipped sideways and crashed during a second flight. Bell quickly figured out why. The airplane needed wingtips that could move, called ailerons, to give the craft stability. So the AEA's next aircraft, the *White Wing*, became the first airplane with ailerons in North America. It also had a three-wheeled undercarriage to make takeoff and landing easier. Baldwin designed this AEA airplane, and all four men flew it in May 1908 until it crashed when hit by a wind gust.

The AEA's third craft was built and flown by Curtiss. The AEA entered Curtiss's *June Bug* in a competition on July 4, 1908— and won. The contest, sponsored by *Scientific American*, was for the first public flight over a kilometer-long course. The *June Bug* not only won, but also went on to fly 150 more times without crashing. "Hurrah for Curtiss! Hurrah for the *June Bug*! Hurrah for the Aerial Association!" telegrammed Alexander Graham Bell to his team.

Selfridge, McCurdy, Curtiss, and Baldwin spent time relaxing at Beinn Bhreagh, too—telling stories, playing billiards, and fencing. Bell's grandson Melville Grosvenor remembered how much fun it was as a boy to watch the test flights in a nearby field, after which "we drove home at night under the stars, Grampy and the AEA boys singing all the way." The four men were like adopted sons of the Bells, so news of an accident involving one of them hit them hard.

This photograph, taken on July 4, 1908, captures Glenn Curtiss in the AEA airplane *June Bug* winning the *Scientific American* trophy for being the first airplane to fly a kilometer in a public demonstration.

Glenn Hammond Curtiss

Glenn Curtiss (1878–1930) was a motorcycle builder, champion racer, and lightweight engine expert when he joined Bell's AEA. After the success of his *June Bug* airplane, Curtiss started his own aircraft company. In 1911, he built the first practical seaplane. The Curtiss Aeroplane and Motor Company received the first contract to build airplanes for the U.S. Navy and built five thousand biplanes for World War I. His best-known plane was the *JN-4*, or "Jenny," a trainer widely used in World War I and later by barnstormers, or stunt pilots.

Glenn Curtiss, shown in this photograph, became an important builder of early airplanes. His most famous model was the *Curtiss Jenny*, the plane shown here.

The Wright brothers, hoping to sell their airplane to the U.S. Army, set up a demonstration to show it off. Selfridge volunteered to be a passenger during the flight. But after a smooth start, a propeller broke and sent the airplane into a nosedive. The impact severely injured Orville Wright and killed Selfridge. Lieutenant Thomas Selfridge became the first person to die in an airplane crash.

This 1908 photograph shows workers trying to free Lieutenant Thomas Selfridge from the wrecked airplane after the crash that killed Selfridge and injured Orville Wright.

"Let's hold tight together, all the tighter for the one that's gone," Mabel Bell wrote to her husband upon learning of Selfridge's death. The other AEA members decided to go ahead and finish up their last airplane in his honor. It was McCurdy who designed the fourth and final AEA airplane, the *Silver Dart*. On February 23, 1909, native Canadian McCurdy piloted his fragile airplane off the ice of Baddeck Bay and flew only a short half-mile flight.

AEA member Douglas McCurdy makes the first airplane flight in Canada piloting the *Silver Dart* off frozen Baddeck Bay near Alexander Graham Bell's Beinn Bhreagh estate.

CHAPTER 12

An Inventor to the Very End

[The inventor] is haunted by an idea. The spirit of invention possesses him, seeking materialization.

"**M**r. Watson, come here. I need you," spoke an aging Alexander Graham Bell into a duplicate of his forty-year-old Centennial Telephone. "It would take me a week to get to you this time," Thomas Watson replied with a smile. Bell was in New York City and Watson in San Francisco that afternoon of January 25, 1915. The two famous men were making a ceremonial telephone call to celebrate the first telephone line to cross the entire North American continent.

"The telephone has gone all over the world. . . . It has grown far beyond my knowledge," Alexander Graham Bell admitted in a speech. "The telephone system as we now know it is the product of many, many minds, to whom honor should be given for the wonderful and beneficial work it has accomplished. I can only say that I am proud and thankful of the fact that it was my crude telephone of 1874–75 that originated the great industry that we see today. . . ." The miraculous accomplishment of the telephone also inspired the invention of the phonograph, helped bring about radio, and paved the way for motion pictures.

Alexander Graham Bell was always a man ahead of his time—and a progressive thinker. He supported women's rights. On his sixty-sixth birthday, he and Mabel cheered

In 1915, Alexander Graham Bell (center) celebrated the success of the first transcontinental telephone line by making a long distance phone call to his assistant, Thomas Watson. Bell, who was in New York, called Watson in San Francisco. This photograph was taken shortly after the phone call

at a Washington, D.C., march for women's voting rights. Bell believed in civil rights for all people and spoke out against the suffocating racism that was commonplace during his lifetime.

Bell never slowed down or stopped experimenting and inventing, either. In a speech he gave in 1891, he explained, "[The inventor] is haunted by an idea. The spirit of invention possesses him, seeking materialization." And so it was with Bell. His inventions had transmitted sounds and combated sickness. His constructions soared through the air and towered over the land. There was only one final element left for Bell to tame—water.

Flying on Water

After the AEA quit flying, the Bells took a round-the-world tour with Casey Baldwin and his wife, Kathleen. While in Italy, the two men met with Enrico Forlanini, the inventor of the hydrofoil. It wasn't a visit they'd soon forget! Forlanini took Bell and Baldwin out on his hydrofoil boat. The men sped "over Lake Maggiore at express train speed," wrote Mabel Bell. Casey Baldwin declared that the high-speed ride was as smooth as flying.

There was only one final element left for Bell to tame—water.

Bell and Baldwin had tinkered with their own hydrofoil designs and model boats back in Nova Scotia. Bell preferred to call the boats hydrodromes, which means "water runners." It related the watercraft to aerodromes, what Bell still insisted on calling airplanes. Bell's Italian boat ride revived the inventor's enthusiasm for hydrofoil design. Once back at Beinn Bhreagh, Bell and Baldwin began building their own boats that fly on water. They ended up building the fastest hydrofoil in the world.

Bell and Baldwin named their hydrofoil the *HD*, an abbreviation for "hydrodrome." Their first full-size hydrofoil, the *HD-1*, reached

This 1913 photograph shows an elderly Alexander Graham Bell writing at his desk in his Washington, D.C., home. Profits from the telephone allowed Bell to work on whatever projects most interested him.

The Hydrofoil

Enrico Forlanini's hydrofoil speeds over Lake Maggiore, Italy, in this photograph. Bell and Casey Baldwin rode on Forlanini's hydrofoil boat in 1911.

A hydrofoil is a boat that lifts its body above the surface of the water when traveling at high speeds. A hydrofoil has wings, called foils, which stay underwater. The foils work like airplane wings; as water rushes past them, they lift the boat out of the water. Hydrofoils also ride smoothly in rough water because the foils reduce the effects of waves.

Italian engineer Enrico Forlanini (1848–1930) invented the hydrofoil around 1900. In 1906, he successfully tested the first full-size, self-propelled hydrofoil. Today commercial hydrofoils carry hundreds of thousands of passengers and many tons of supplies and equipment each year. The military also uses high-speed hydrofoils.

a respectable speed of thirty miles per hour (mph). By the *HD-3*, the boats were streaking across Baddeck Bay at fifty mph. By 1919, Baldwin and Bell had built a huge, streamlined hydrofoil called the *HD-4*. This sleek, sixty-foot-long boat was shaped like a torpedo with wings. The U.S. Navy had rejected Bell's *HD* design a few years earlier. But with World War I over, they sent Bell two big engines to test. These 350-horsepower

Bell and Baldwin hoped they'd make the HD-4 the fastest boat in the world.

Alexander Graham Bell (right), Casey Baldwin (left), and Baldwin's young son Robert (center) are aboard the *HD-4* hydrofoil boat on Bras d'Or Lake, Cape Breton Island, in this 1919 photograph.

engines powered two aerial propellers that boosted the boat's speed. Bell and Baldwin hoped they'd make the *HD-4* the fastest boat in the world.

On September 9, 1919, the *HD-4* began moving across Baddeck Bay. It was another ride to remember. "At fifteen knots (seventeen mph) you feel the machine rising bodily out of the water," wrote one witness. "[O]nce up and clear of the drag [of water] she drives ahead with an acceleration that makes you grip your seat to keep from being left behind. The wind on your face is like the pressure of a giant hand and an occasional dash of fine spray stings like birdshot. . . . It's unbelievable—it defies the laws of physics, but it's true." The *HD-4* set a world's marine speed record that day when it flew atop the water at an unbelievable 70.86 mph. The record would remain unbroken for ten years. But Alexander Graham Bell never personally rode in the *HD-4*. He just didn't feel up to it. Bell suffered from **diabetes**. And the disease was weakening his health.

Life and Legacy

By late July 1922, Alexander Graham Bell became seriously ill. He died a few days later, on August 2, at age seventy-five. Mabel was at her husband's side when he passed away at his beloved Beinn Bhreagh estate. The inventor was laid in a simple pine coffin, made by his workmen and lined with leftover kite fabric. A large rock serves as the grave marker of Alexander and Mabel, who died only five months later. Under Alexander Graham Bell's name, it simply reads: INVENTOR • TEACHER. At the time of Bell's burial, all telephone service in Canada and the United States was stopped for one minute in honor of the inventor.

"We are all too much inclined, I think, to walk through life with our eyes closed . . . ," Alexander Graham Bell wrote in a 1918 article.

OBSERVATION: TWIN BROTHER TO INVENTION

The only copy we have
Observations of Experiments
No. 9

By Alexander Graham Bell

DID you ever put your head under water and knock two stones together to find out what the sound is like?

If you have never done that, try it and you will get a new sensation. I did it once, and it ...unded as if a man were hammering at my very ear. I then took two tiny pebbles and tapped them lightly together under the water. It sounded like a man knocking at the door. I was rather startled to hear such a loud noise from such a slight cause, and of course the question at once came to my mind: How far away could I hear the sound?

So I sent a boy a couple of hundred feet up the beach, and directed him to strike two stones together under the water. When I submerged my head I could hear the sound as readily as before. Then, determining to try the maximum possible distance, I sent the boy across the bay in a boat, to a point at least a mile away from where I stood. Through my field glass I saw him land on the other side, go down to a little plank wharf, lie face downward upon the wharf and put his hands into the water. I then knew that he was signalling with the stones.

Slipping into the water on my side of the bay, I submerged my head and listened intently. Clear and perfectly distinct the signals came to my ear through more than a mile of water! It was an astonishing revelation of what can be done with water. In air, sound travels about a thousand feet a second; but in water it goes five times as fast as that—about five thousand feet a second—because water is a much better conductor than air.

In reasoning upon these experiments the thought occurred to me: If two little stones tapped together under the water make such a big sound, every tiny lobster that snaps his claws must make an audible click. Are there, I asked myself, creatures in the water that signal to one another by sound?

I had occasion once to make the experiment. While bathing in the Grand River in Ontario, I put my hand very gently under the water and listened. Tick! tick! came a sound from one side like the clicking of a grasshopper, followed by a similar chirrup from the other side. Evidently there were creatures under the water calling to one another. I do not know whether all fish make sounds or not, but there are certainly some fish that do. The drumfish on our coast, for example, drums away in the water so loud that he can often be heard on the shore. It is also a significant fact that fish have ears. Why should they have those organs if there is nothing for them to hear?

Therefore, of this we may be certain: there is a whole world of sound beneath the waves waiting to be explored.

We are all too much inclined, I think, to walk through life with our eyes closed. There are things round us and all at our very feet that we have never seen, because we have never really looked. We should not keep forever on the public road, going only where others have gone; we should leave the beaten track occasionally and turn the woods. Every time you do that you will be certain to find something that you have never seen before. Of course, it will be a little thing; but do not ignore it. Follow it up, explore all round it; one discovery will lead to another, and before you know it you will have something worth thinking about to occupy your mind, for all really big discoveries are the results of thought.

Let us return to the experiment of knocking the stones together under the water and think about it.

Why should we not simply put an ear to the water instead of submerging the whole head? Why should we not ring a bell under the water, instead of clicking stones together to make a noise? An ordinary dinner bell would do. Empty it of air and ring it under the water, and a person with his ear submerged can hear it at a great distance. But would it not be better to transmit the sound vibrations from the water to the ear through some intervening mechanism and thus obviate the necessity of submerging the ear at all?

I have tried submerged hearing tubes of various kinds and plates partly submerged, with the ear applied to the part out of the water. If you put your ear to the bottom of a boat—inside, of course—you can readily hear a bell ring under the water some distance away. Still better, fasten a telephone transmitter to the bottom of the boat and put an oil at one end with the telephone receiver at your ear. Or you may put the transmitter overboard. It then becomes a submerged ear and will listen for you under the water. That is the principle of the submarine signaling that is now in use on many large commercial and naval vessels.

Alexander Graham Bell recognized as one of the eminent men of science of modern times, is best known as the inventor of the telephone

On these ships the telephone transmitters are attached to the thin iron skin of the hull and the receiving telephone is on the bridge. On shore there are huge bells at lighthouse stations making underwater fog signals that a steamer ten miles away can pick up. It is doubtful whether a fog signal could be heard through the air at any such distance. The air in air is not a poor conductor of sound, and it affords many chances for illusions of hearing. For example, an island casts a "sound shadow" upon the water. The sound wave striking the island is deflected into the sky, and a person would have to be up in a balloon to hear it, for it might not come down again to the surface for a mile or two beyond the island. A ship close to the island may, therefore, not hear the signal at all, until too late to avoid running aground.

The transmitting qualities of the air are likewise subject to variations on account of unusual atmospheric conditions. You may be near a fog station and yet hear the sound so faintly that it seems to be far away. The sounds echo from the clouds or from the walls of a ship and thus add other puzzling aspects to the problem.

There is always room for investigating new, for the list of investigations is far from being closed. Consider, for example, the ramifications suggested by the transmission of sound through water.

Three-quarters of the earth's surface is submerged and has not yet been explored to any great degree. The only way we have of reaching the mountains and valleys at the bottom of the sea is by sending down a sounding line and turning up a specimen of the bottom attached to the sinker. It is not easy, however, to reach the bed of the sea through a mile or two miles of water and it requires several hours to take a single sounding. It is therefore expensive both in time and in labor to ascertain the depth of the ocean.

Why not send down a sound instead and listen for the echo from the bottom? Knowing the velocity of sound in water and the time taken for the echo to reach the ear, we should be able to ascertain the depth of the deepest part of the ocean. Here is an idea that would seem to be worth trying. I have suggested it several times, but I do not know that it has ever been acted upon. The experiment might reveal not only the depth of the ocean but something of the na-

In this 1918 article, Alexander Graham Bell describes his belief that it is important to always look for new discoveries in life. This attitude led him to be a great inventor.

"We should not keep forever on the public road, going only where others have gone; we should leave the beaten track occasionally and enter the woods. Every time you do that you will be certain to find something that you have never seen before. . . . Follow it up, explore all around it; one discovery will lead to another, and before you know it you will have something worth thinking about to occupy your mind, for all really big discoveries are the results of thought."

Glossary

apparatus—a piece of machinery, or a device.

caveat—a confidential, formal declaration stating an intention to file a patent on an in-progress invention.

centennial—a hundredth anniversary of an event.

context—the information surrounding a word that helps determine its meaning.

criterion—a standard on which a judgment or decision is based (the plural form is *criteria*).

diabetes—a medical condition, also called diabetes mellitus, in which the body produces an insufficient amount of insulin, causing elevated blood sugar.

ear tube—a horn- or funnel-shaped device, also called an ear trumpet, used to direct sound into the ear of a partially deaf person.

eardrum—the thin membrane in the ear that carries sound waves as vibrations; it's also called the tympanic membrane or tympanum.

electromagnetism—the scientific study of the interaction of electrical and magnetic fields.

Gaelic—the ancient language of the Celts in Ireland and Scotland.

infringing—failing to obey or follow a legal contract or patent.

membrane—a thin, flexible sheet of material that covers or divides something.

monopoly—the complete control over the entire supply of goods or a service in a certain market by a single company or group.

receivers—devices for changing electrical impulses into sound.

respirator—a machine that maintains breathing.

scarlet fever—a contagious bacterial infection, also called scarlatina, that mainly affects children and causes fever, swelling, pain in the nose, throat, and mouth, and a red rash.

transmitters—devices that convert sound waves to electrical impulses.

ultimatum—a demand accompanied by a threat.

vocal cords—strips of tissue in the larynx that produce sound by vibrating.

vocal physiology—the study of how the vocal organs produce sound and speech.

Bibliography

Bell, Alexander Graham. "Discovery and Invention." *National Geographic Magazine* (June 1914): Vol. 25, no. 6, pp. 649–655.

Bell, Alexander Graham. "Prehistoric Telephone Days." *National Geographic Magazine* (March 1922): Vol. 41, no. 3, pp. 223–241.

Bruce, Robert V. *Bell: Alexander Graham Bell and Conquest of Solitude.* Ithaca, NY: Cornell University Press, 1973.

Foster, Tony. *The Sound and the Silence: The Private Lives of Mabel and Alexander Graham Bell.* Halifax, Nova Scotia: Nimbus, 1996.

Grosvenor, Edwin S., and Morgan Wesson. *Alexander Graham Bell: The Life and Times of the Man Who Invented the Telephone.* New York: Harry N. Abrams, 1997.

Keller, Helen. *The Story of My Life.* New York: Norton, 2003.

Waite, Helen Elmira. *Make a Joyful Sound: The Romance of Mabel Hubbard and Alexander Graham Bell.* Philadelphia: Macrae Smith Company, 1961

Watson, Thomas A. *Exploring Life: The Autobiography of Thomas A. Watson.* New York: Appleton, 1926.

Image Credits

About the Author

Mary Kay Carson began her writing career working on a classroom science magazine fifteen years ago. She's now the author of more than twenty nonfiction books for kids and teachers about space, weather, nature, and other science and history topics. Recent titles include *Emi and the Rhino Scientist* and *Exploring the Solar System*. Carson lives in Cincinnati, Ohio. (For more, visit: www.marykaycarson.com.)

Index